Mometrix TEST PREPARATION

M-STEP

Grade 8

English Language Arts

I0878895

Dear Future Exam Success Story

First of all, **THANK YOU** for purchasing Mometrix study materials!

Second, congratulations! You are one of the few determined test-takers who are committed to doing whatever it takes to excel on your exam. **You have come to the right place.** We developed these study materials with one goal in mind: to deliver you the information you need in a format that's concise and easy to use.

In addition to optimizing your guide for the content of the test, we've outlined our recommended steps for breaking down the preparation process into small, attainable goals so you can make sure you stay on track.

We've also analyzed the entire test-taking process, identifying the most common pitfalls and showing how you can overcome them and be ready for any curveball the test throws you.

Standardized testing is one of the biggest obstacles on your road to success, which only increases the importance of doing well in the high-pressure, high-stakes environment of test day. Your results on this test could have a significant impact on your future, and this guide provides the information and practical advice to help you achieve your full potential on test day.

Your success is our success

We would love to hear from you! If you would like to share the story of your exam success or if you have any questions or comments in regard to our products, please contact us at **800-673-8175** or **support@mometrix.com**.

Thanks again for your business and we wish you continued success!

Sincerely,
The Mometrix Test Preparation Team

Written and edited by the Mometrix Test Preparation Team
Printed in the United States of America

Table of Contents

Introduction

Thank you for purchasing this resource! You have made the choice to prepare yourself for a test that could have a huge impact on your future, and this guide is designed to help you be fully ready for test day. Obviously, it's important to have a solid understanding of the test material, but you also need to be prepared for the unique environment and stressors of the test, so that you can perform to the best of your abilities.

For this purpose, the first section that appears in this guide is the **Success Strategies**. We've devoted countless hours to meticulously researching what works and what doesn't, and we've boiled down our findings to the most impactful steps you can take to improve your performance on the test. We start at the beginning with study planning and move through the preparation process, all the way to the testing strategies that will help you get the most out of what you know when you're finally sitting in front of the test.

We recommend that you start preparing for your test as far in advance as possible. However, if you've bought this guide as a last-minute study resource and only have a few days before your test, we recommend that you skip over the first two Success Strategies since they address a long-term study plan.

If you struggle with **test anxiety**, we strongly encourage you to check out our recommendations for how you can overcome it. Test anxiety is a formidable foe, but it can be beaten, and we want to make sure you have the tools you need to defeat it.

Strategy #1 – Plan Big, Study Small

There's a lot riding on your performance. If you want to ace this test, you're going to need to keep your skills sharp and the material fresh in your mind. You need a plan that lets you review everything you need to know while still fitting in your schedule. We'll break this strategy down into three categories.

Information Organization

Start with the information you already have: the official test outline. From this, you can make a complete list of all the concepts you need to cover before the test. Organize these concepts into groups that can be studied together, and create a list of any related vocabulary you need to learn so you can brush up on any difficult terms. You'll want to keep this vocabulary list handy once you actually start studying since you may need to add to it along the way.

Time Management

Once you have your set of study concepts, decide how to spread them out over the time you have left before the test. Break your study plan into small, clear goals so you have a manageable task for each day and know exactly what you're doing. Then just focus on one small step at a time. When you manage your time this way, you don't need to spend hours at a time studying. Studying a small block of content for a short period each day helps you retain information better and avoid stressing over how much you have left to do. You can relax knowing that you have a plan to cover everything in time. In order for this strategy to be effective though, you have to start studying early and stick to your schedule. Avoid the exhaustion and futility that comes from last-minute cramming!

Study Environment

The environment you study in has a big impact on your learning. Studying in a coffee shop, while probably more enjoyable, is not likely to be as fruitful as studying in a quiet room. It's important to keep distractions to a minimum. You're only planning to study for a short block of time, so make the most of it. Don't pause to check your phone or get up to find a snack. It's also important to **avoid multitasking**. Research has consistently shown that multitasking will make your studying dramatically less effective. Your study area should also be comfortable and well-lit so you don't have the distraction of straining your eyes or sitting on an uncomfortable chair.

The time of day you study is also important. You want to be rested and alert. Don't wait until just before bedtime. Study when you'll be most likely to comprehend and remember. Even better, if you know what time of day your test will be, set that time aside for study. That way your brain will be used to working on that subject at that specific time and you'll have a better chance of recalling information.

Finally, it can be helpful to team up with others who are studying for the same test. Your actual studying should be done in as isolated an environment as possible, but the work of organizing the information and setting up the study plan can be divided up. In between study sessions, you can discuss with your teammates the concepts that you're all studying and quiz each other on the details. Just be sure that your teammates are as serious about the test as you are. If you find that your study time is being replaced with social time, you might need to find a new team.

Strategy #2 – Make Your Studying Count

You're devoting a lot of time and effort to preparing for this test, so you want to be absolutely certain it will pay off. This means doing more than just reading the content and hoping you can remember it on test day. It's important to make every minute of study count. There are two main areas you can focus on to make your studying count.

Retention

It doesn't matter how much time you study if you can't remember the material. You need to make sure you are retaining the concepts. To check your retention of the information you're learning, try recalling it at later times with minimal prompting. Try carrying around flashcards and glance at one or two from time to time or ask a friend who's also studying for the test to quiz you.

To enhance your retention, look for ways to put the information into practice so that you can apply it rather than simply recalling it. If you're using the information in practical ways, it will be much easier to remember. Similarly, it helps to solidify a concept in your mind if you're not only reading it to yourself but also explaining it to someone else. Ask a friend to let you teach them about a concept you're a little shaky on (or speak aloud to an imaginary audience if necessary). As you try to summarize, define, give examples, and answer your friend's questions, you'll understand the concepts better and they will stay with you longer. Finally, step back for a big picture view and ask yourself how each piece of information fits with the whole subject. When you link the different concepts together and see them working together as a whole, it's easier to remember the individual components.

Finally, practice showing your work on any multi-step problems, even if you're just studying. Writing out each step you take to solve a problem will help solidify the process in your mind, and you'll be more likely to remember it during the test.

Modality

Modality simply refers to the means or method by which you study. Choosing a study modality that fits your own individual learning style is crucial. No two people learn best in exactly the same way, so it's important to know your strengths and use them to your advantage.

For example, if you learn best by visualization, focus on visualizing a concept in your mind and draw an image or a diagram. Try color-coding your notes, illustrating them, or creating symbols that will trigger your mind to recall a learned concept. If you learn best by hearing or discussing information, find a study partner who learns the same way or read aloud to yourself. Think about how to put the information in your own words. Imagine that you are giving a lecture on the topic and record yourself so you can listen to it later.

For any learning style, flashcards can be helpful. Organize the information so you can take advantage of spare moments to review. Underline key words or phrases. Use different colors for different categories. Mnemonic devices (such as creating a short list in which every item starts with the same letter) can also help with retention. Find what works best for you and use it to store the information in your mind most effectively and easily.

Strategy #3 – Practice the Right Way

Your success on test day depends not only on how many hours you put into preparing, but also on whether you prepared the right way. It's good to check along the way to see if your studying is paying off. One of the most effective ways to do this is by taking practice tests to evaluate your progress. Practice tests are useful because they show exactly where you need to improve. Every time you take a practice test, pay special attention to these three groups of questions:

- The questions you got wrong
- The questions you had to guess on, even if you guessed right
- The questions you found difficult or slow to work through

This will show you exactly what your weak areas are, and where you need to devote more study time. Ask yourself why each of these questions gave you trouble. Was it because you didn't understand the material? Was it because you didn't remember the vocabulary? Do you need more repetitions on this type of question to build speed and confidence? Dig into those questions and figure out how you can strengthen your weak areas as you go back to review the material.

Additionally, many practice tests have a section explaining the answer choices. It can be tempting to read the explanation and think that you now have a good understanding of the concept. However, an explanation likely only covers part of the question's broader context. Even if the explanation makes perfect sense, **go back and investigate** every concept related to the question until you're positive you have a thorough understanding.

As you go along, keep in mind that the practice test is just that: practice. Memorizing these questions and answers will not be very helpful on the actual test because it is unlikely to have any of the same exact questions. If you only know the right answers to the sample questions, you won't be prepared for the real thing. **Study the concepts** until you understand them fully, and then you'll be able to answer any question that shows up on the test.

It's important to wait on the practice tests until you're ready. If you take a test on your first day of study, you may be overwhelmed by the amount of material covered and how much you need to learn. Work up to it gradually.

On test day, you'll need to be prepared for answering questions, managing your time, and using the test-taking strategies you've learned. It's a lot to balance, like a mental marathon that will have a big impact on your future. Like training for a marathon, you'll need to start slowly and work your way up. When test day arrives, you'll be ready.

Start with the strategies you've read in the first two Success Strategies—plan your course and study in the way that works best for you. If you have time, consider using multiple study resources to get different approaches to the same concepts. It can be helpful to see difficult concepts from more than one angle. Then find a good source for practice tests. Many times, the test website will suggest potential study resources or provide sample tests.

Practice Test Strategy

If you're able to find at least three practice tests, we recommend this strategy:

UNTIMED AND OPEN-BOOK PRACTICE

Take the first test with no time constraints and with your notes and study guide handy. Take your time and focus on applying the strategies you've learned.

TIMED AND OPEN-BOOK PRACTICE

Take the second practice test open-book as well, but set a timer and practice pacing yourself to finish in time.

TIMED AND CLOSED-BOOK PRACTICE

Take any other practice tests as if it were test day. Set a timer and put away your study materials. Sit at a table or desk in a quiet room, imagine yourself at the testing center, and answer questions as quickly and accurately as possible.

Keep repeating timed and closed-book tests on a regular basis until you run out of practice tests or it's time for the actual test. Your mind will be ready for the schedule and stress of test day, and you'll be able to focus on recalling the material you've learned.

Strategy #4 – Pace Yourself

Once you're fully prepared for the material on the test, your biggest challenge on test day will be managing your time. Just knowing that the clock is ticking can make you panic even if you have plenty of time left. Work on pacing yourself so you can build confidence against the time constraints of the exam. Pacing is a difficult skill to master, especially in a high-pressure environment, so **practice is vital**.

Set time expectations for your pace based on how much time is available. For example, if a section has 60 questions and the time limit is 30 minutes, you know you have to average 30 seconds or less per question in order to answer them all. Although 30 seconds is the hard limit, set 25 seconds per question as your goal, so you reserve extra time to spend on harder questions. When you budget extra time for the harder questions, you no longer have any reason to stress when those questions take longer to answer.

Don't let this time expectation distract you from working through the test at a calm, steady pace, but keep it in mind so you don't spend too much time on any one question. Recognize that taking extra time on one question you don't understand may keep you from answering two that you do understand later in the test. If your time limit for a question is up and you're still not sure of the answer, mark it and move on, and come back to it later if the time and the test format allow. If the testing format doesn't allow you to return to earlier questions, just make an educated guess; then put it out of your mind and move on.

On the easier questions, be careful not to rush. It may seem wise to hurry through them so you have more time for the challenging ones, but it's not worth missing one if you know the concept and just didn't take the time to read the question fully. Work efficiently but make sure you understand the question and have looked at all of the answer choices, since more than one may seem right at first.

Even if you're paying attention to the time, you may find yourself a little behind at some point. You should speed up to get back on track, but do so wisely. Don't panic; just take a few seconds less on each question until you're caught up. Don't guess without thinking, but do look through the answer choices and eliminate any you know are wrong. If you can get down to two choices, it is often worthwhile to guess from those. Once you've chosen an answer, move on and don't dwell on any that you skipped or had to hurry through. If a question was taking too long, chances are it was one of the harder ones, so you weren't as likely to get it right anyway.

On the other hand, if you find yourself getting ahead of schedule, it may be beneficial to slow down a little. The more quickly you work, the more likely you are to make a careless mistake that will affect your score. You've budgeted time for each question, so don't be afraid to spend that time. Practice an efficient but careful pace to get the most out of the time you have.

Test-Taking Strategies

This section contains a list of test-taking strategies that you may find helpful as you work through the test. By taking what you know and applying logical thought, you can maximize your chances of answering any question correctly!

It is very important to realize that every question is different and every person is different: no single strategy will work on every question, and no single strategy will work for every person. That's why we've included all of them here, so you can try them out and determine which ones work best for different types of questions and which ones work best for you.

Question Strategies

☑ Read Carefully

Read the question and the answer choices carefully. Don't miss the question because you misread the terms. You have plenty of time to read each question thoroughly and make sure you understand what is being asked. Yet a happy medium must be attained, so don't waste too much time. You must read carefully and efficiently.

☑ Contextual Clues

Look for contextual clues. If the question includes a word you are not familiar with, look at the immediate context for some indication of what the word might mean. Contextual clues can often give you all the information you need to decipher the meaning of an unfamiliar word. Even if you can't determine the meaning, you may be able to narrow down the possibilities enough to make a solid guess at the answer to the question.

☑ Prefixes

If you're having trouble with a word in the question or answer choices, try dissecting it. Take advantage of every clue that the word might include. Prefixes can be a huge help. Usually, they allow you to determine a basic meaning. *Pre-* means before, *post-* means after, *pro-* is positive, *de-* is negative. From prefixes, you can get an idea of the general meaning of the word and try to put it into context.

☑ Hedge Words

Watch out for critical hedge words, such as *likely, may, can, often, almost, mostly, usually, generally, rarely*, and *sometimes*. Question writers insert these hedge phrases to cover every possibility. Often an answer choice will be wrong simply because it leaves no room for exception. Be on guard for answer choices that have definitive words such as *exactly* and *always*.

☑ Switchback Words

Stay alert for *switchbacks*. These are the words and phrases frequently used to alert you to shifts in thought. The most common switchback words are *but, although*, and *however*. Others include *nevertheless, on the other hand, even though, while, in spite of, despite*, and *regardless of*. Switchback words are important to catch because they can change the direction of the question or an answer choice.

☑ Face Value

When in doubt, use common sense. Accept the situation in the problem at face value. Don't read too much into it. These problems will not require you to make wild assumptions. If you have to go beyond creativity and warp time or space in order to have an answer choice fit the question, then you should move on and consider the other answer choices. These are normal problems rooted in reality. The applicable relationship or explanation may not be readily apparent, but it is there for you to figure out. Use your common sense to interpret anything that isn't clear.

Answer Choice Strategies

☑ Answer Selection

The most thorough way to pick an answer choice is to identify and eliminate wrong answers until only one is left, then confirm it is the correct answer. Sometimes an answer choice may immediately seem right, but be careful. The test writers will usually put more than one reasonable answer choice on each question, so take a second to read all of them and make sure that the other choices are not equally obvious. As long as you have time left, it is better to read every answer choice than to pick the first one that looks right without checking the others.

☑ Answer Choice Families

An answer choice family consists of two (in rare cases, three) answer choices that are very similar in construction and cannot all be true at the same time. If you see two answer choices that are direct opposites or parallels, one of them is usually the correct answer. For instance, if one answer choice says that quantity *x* increases and another either says that quantity *x* decreases (opposite) or says that quantity *y* increases (parallel), then those answer choices would fall into the same family. An answer choice that doesn't match the construction of the answer choice family is more likely to be incorrect. Most questions will not have answer choice families, but when they do appear, you should be prepared to recognize them.

☑ Eliminate Answers

Eliminate answer choices as soon as you realize they are wrong, but make sure you consider all possibilities. If you are eliminating answer choices and realize that the last one you are left with is also wrong, don't panic. Start over and consider each choice again. There may be something you missed the first time that you will realize on the second pass.

☑ Avoid Fact Traps

Don't be distracted by an answer choice that is factually true but doesn't answer the question. You are looking for the choice that answers the question. Stay focused on what the question is asking for so you don't accidentally pick an answer that is true but incorrect. Always go back to the question and make sure the answer choice you've selected actually answers the question and is not merely a true statement.

☑ Extreme Statements

In general, you should avoid answers that put forth extreme actions as standard practice or proclaim controversial ideas as established fact. An answer choice that states the "process should be used in certain situations, if..." is much more likely to be correct than one that states the "process should be discontinued completely." The first is a calm rational statement and doesn't even make a definitive, uncompromising stance, using a hedge word *if* to provide wiggle room, whereas the second choice is far more extreme.

⊘ Benchmark

As you read through the answer choices and you come across one that seems to answer the question well, mentally select that answer choice. This is not your final answer, but it's the one that will help you evaluate the other answer choices. The one that you selected is your benchmark or standard for judging each of the other answer choices. Every other answer choice must be compared to your benchmark. That choice is correct until proven otherwise by another answer choice beating it. If you find a better answer, then that one becomes your new benchmark. Once you've decided that no other choice answers the question as well as your benchmark, you have your final answer.

⊘ Predict the Answer

Before you even start looking at the answer choices, it is often best to try to predict the answer. When you come up with the answer on your own, it is easier to avoid distractions and traps because you will know exactly what to look for. The right answer choice is unlikely to be word-for-word what you came up with, but it should be a close match. Even if you are confident that you have the right answer, you should still take the time to read each option before moving on.

General Strategies

⊘ Tough Questions

If you are stumped on a problem or it appears too hard or too difficult, don't waste time. Move on! Remember though, if you can quickly check for obviously incorrect answer choices, your chances of guessing correctly are greatly improved. Before you completely give up, at least try to knock out a couple of possible answers. Eliminate what you can and then guess at the remaining answer choices before moving on.

⊘ Check Your Work

Since you will probably not know every term listed and the answer to every question, it is important that you get credit for the ones that you do know. Don't miss any questions through careless mistakes. If at all possible, try to take a second to look back over your answer selection and make sure you've selected the correct answer choice and haven't made a costly careless mistake (such as marking an answer choice that you didn't mean to mark). This quick double check should more than pay for itself in caught mistakes for the time it costs.

⊘ Pace Yourself

It's easy to be overwhelmed when you're looking at a page full of questions; your mind is confused and full of random thoughts, and the clock is ticking down faster than you would like. Calm down and maintain the pace that you have set for yourself. Especially as you get down to the last few minutes of the test, don't let the small numbers on the clock make you panic. As long as you are on track by monitoring your pace, you are guaranteed to have time for each question.

⊘ Don't Rush

It is very easy to make errors when you are in a hurry. Maintaining a fast pace in answering questions is pointless if it makes you miss questions that you would have gotten right otherwise. Test writers like to include distracting information and wrong answers that seem right. Taking a little extra time to avoid careless mistakes can make all the difference in your test score. Find a pace that allows you to be confident in the answers that you select.

⊘ Keep Moving

Panicking will not help you pass the test, so do your best to stay calm and keep moving. Taking deep breaths and going through the answer elimination steps you practiced can help to break through a stress barrier and keep your pace.

Final Notes

The combination of a solid foundation of content knowledge and the confidence that comes from practicing your plan for applying that knowledge is the key to maximizing your performance on test day. As your foundation of content knowledge is built up and strengthened, you'll find that the strategies included in this chapter become more and more effective in helping you quickly sift through the distractions and traps of the test to isolate the correct answer.

Now that you're preparing to move forward into the test content chapters of this book, be sure to keep your goal in mind. As you read, think about how you will be able to apply this information on the test. If you've already seen sample questions for the test and you have an idea of the question format and style, try to come up with questions of your own that you can answer based on what you're reading. This will give you valuable practice applying your knowledge in the same ways you can expect to on test day.

Good luck and good studying!

English Language Arts

The Writing Process

Brainstorming

When choosing what to write about, activities like brainstorming can help inspire new ideas or help writers see how their ideas go together. **Brainstorming** means considering a variety of topics or ideas and is mainly used to find a creative approach to a subject or problem. A good first step in brainstorming is simple **free-association** with a topic. One way of doing this is sitting down with paper and pen and writing every thought that comes to mind about the topic in a word or phrase. It does not matter how helpful or good the thought seems at first; the writer should write down everything that comes to mind about the topic. Then, the writer should read the list over a few times. Next, he or she should look for patterns, repetitions, and clusters of ideas. This allows a variety of fresh ideas to come as the writer thinks about the topic.

Free Writing

Free writing is a more organized form of brainstorming. **Free writing** means taking a limited amount of time, like 2 to 3 minutes, to write everything that comes to mind about a topic in complete sentences. When the time is up, the writer should review everything he or she has written down. Many of the sentences may not make sense, but they may contain ideas and details that help the writer organize his or her ideas and prepare to plan the composition. Usually, free writing results in more useful ideas than brainstorming because the writer's thoughts and connections are written in complete sentences. However, both methods can be used together to help the writer prepare to plan and write a composition.

Mapping

One specific way to use graphic organizers is to map an essay. There are many different types of graphic organizers. One easy method to create one is to draw a circle in the middle of the page and write a broad topic in it. Then, draw smaller circles with related topics and ideas, or with topics that fit within the broad topic, written inside and draw line to connect each circle to the main circle. This method can show ideas that fit within the broad topic and will help guide the essay, or it can show which ideas may work better as the main topic of the essay.

Once the main idea and other ideas and details for the essay have been chosen, they can be used to map the essay. Mapping is another word for using a certain type of graphic organizer. These graphic organizers look like a map and organize ideas and details as they will appear in the essay. The essay map can have the main idea at the top or in the center. If the main idea is at the top, the supporting ideas will appear below it in a row, and any additional details will appear under the supporting idea they go with. If the main idea appears in the center, the supporting ideas may appear around it, and the additional details will appear around the supporting ideas they go with.

Planning

Planning is the process of organizing a piece of writing before writing a draft. At the beginning of planning, writers should decide **why they are writing** and **who will read what they write**. The writer must also choose a **genre**, which is the **type** of composition he or she will write. There are fiction genres, such as comedy, folklore, action, and mystery. There are also nonfiction genres, such as essays, reports, poems, and journals. To plan his or her composition, a writer may create an outline or a graphic organizer, such as a Venn diagram, a spider-map, or a flowchart. These methods should help the writer choose their topic, main ideas, and how to organize the composition. If the writer needs to do research for the composition, he or she may also do so as they plan. Planning helps writers organize all of their ideas and decide if they have enough information to begin their first draft. However, writers should remember that the decisions they make during planning may change later, so their plan does not have to be perfect.

Drafting

Writers may then use their plan, outline, or graphic organizer to compose their first draft. They may write more drafts after the first one to improve their writing. Writing multiple drafts can help writers think of different ways to state their ideas and correct mistakes that may be hard to fix without rewriting a section of the composition, or the whole composition. There is no "right" number of drafts, so different writers may write a different number of drafts. Writing drafts also makes it easier to write freely because a writer can improve his or her composition with each draft they write.

Revising, Editing, and Proofreading

Once a writer completes a draft, he or she can move on to revising, editing, and proofreading to improve the draft. **Revising** is making sure that the composition is right for the audience, is not missing important information, is on topic, and is well organized. The writer should also consider the composition's style when revising and ensure that it is appropriately formal or serious. Revising may happen after the first draft so that errors are not repeated in the next draft. Each draft should be revised before the next one is written so that no mistakes are missed. **Editing** comes next. Editing a composition includes steps like improving transitions between paragraphs and making sure each paragraph is on topic. While editing, the writer must pay attention to the words he or she uses and the way the information in each paragraph is organized. Writers may also fix grammar mistakes in the editing phase, since some errors will require a writer to rewrite large parts of their work. **Proofreading** means fixing misspelled words, errors in grammar, and any other small mistakes in the composition.

During the revising, editing, and proofreading steps, it can be helpful for writers to ask a peer to read their work, since he or she may notice mistakes or problems the writer missed before. A writer may also choose to read his or her own work aloud, or listen to someone else read it. Hearing a composition aloud can help writers find mistakes or opportunities for improvement in their work more easily. This happens because when something is read aloud, the person reading the text must pay closer attention to the words on the page. When a writer or a peer reads the composition, they should point out any sentence that confuses them the first time they read it. Most of these sentences can be revised in a way that makes it easier to read and understand.

Adding and Removing Information

While both revising and editing may involve changing the words in a composition, they can also involve adding or taking away words. When a writer has completed a draft and reread it, he or she may notice that something, such as a transition, important details, or an explanatory sentence, is missing. Simply changing the words to make the passage sound better will not solve this problem, so the writer must **add** whatever words and information is needed to make the passage make sense and achieve the writer's purpose.

In other cases, a writer may have words, a sentence, or sometimes an entire paragraph that gives unnecessary information or explains the information in a way that is confusing. When this happens, the extra words and information weaken the composition and must be **removed**. Sometimes, this is difficult for writers to do because it may require them to remove writing they are proud of or a fact they find interesting. Despite this, revising and editing are steps meant to improve and strengthen a composition, so the writer should change, add, or remove parts of his or her writing in a way that makes it better and achieves his or her purpose.

Revising Sentences

Sentence variety is important to consider when writing an essay. A variety of sentence lengths and types can make an essay more engaging, and different types of sentences can sometimes help readers better understand information. For example, a sentence containing a list may make more sense when written with a simple sentence structure, since writing a compound sentence containing a list may give the reader too much information at once. On the other hand, information that is closely related and can be connected with a conjunction should be written in a compound sentence, rather than a simple sentence, since a compound sentence helps the reader see that the information goes together.

Using only simple sentences often makes writing boring and bothersome to read. Writing using only compound sentences makes it difficult for writers to explain information well and difficult for readers to understand, since every sentence will include a coordinating conjunction. To check an essay for sentence variety, it is helpful to look at whether the essay contains different sentence structures and lengths. It is also important to pay attention to the way each sentence starts and avoid beginning with the same words or phrases.

Revising Vocabulary

When writing informational or argumentative texts, it is important to use **precise vocabulary**, or **word choice**, to explain your main idea and supporting details. Generalized vocabulary will not help the audience fully understand the points that you are attempting to make because it will not accurately explain your main idea and supporting details. Precise vocabulary is important to use because it will accurately describe the ideas that are central to your text. When you research a subject, make sure to familiarize yourself with any vocabulary that is involved in its explanation. Use context clues, dictionaries, or, if necessary, a technical dictionary to decode any words that you are not familiar with. Precise vocabulary also impacts the effectiveness of narrative text. Carefully choosing vocabulary to describe sensory details, or imagery, helps writers paint the best possible picture of the events they are describing through their writing.

Recursive Writing Process

Brainstorming, planning, drafting, revising, editing, and proofreading are all steps in the **writing process**. This process is helpful to remember when beginning a new composition, but once a writer has practiced these steps in this order, he or she can use the **recursive writing process**. The recursive writing process is the same as the normal writing process, but the steps in the recursive writing process do not have to happen in the same order. For example, one writer may need to repeat steps after completing other steps. A different writer may discover that he or she can practice the planning and revising steps as he or she writes a draft. The recursive writing process involves moving back and forth between planning, drafting, and revising, followed by more planning, more drafting, and more revising until the writer is happy with his or her work. Each writer can use the recursive writing process in their own way, as long as it helps them improve their work and write the best they can.

Review Video: Recursive Writing Process
Visit mometrix.com/academy and enter code: 951611

Essay Structure and Organization

Central Ideas and Supporting Details

In the first paragraph of a composition, writers include a sentence that explains the **central idea.** This sentence is also known as the **thesis**. The rest of the paragraph shows the reader why the topic of the essay is interesting and includes details that support the central idea. One way to understand the relationship between the central idea and supporting information is to think about a table: the tabletop is the central idea, and each of the table's legs is a supporting detail or group of details. All of the legs work together to support the tabletop and create a table, just like the supporting details work together to support the central idea and create a composition.

Introduction

The introduction is used to capture the reader's attention and announce the essay's central idea. Normally, the introduction contains about 3-5 sentences. An introduction can begin with an interesting quote, a question, a strong opinion, or something else that will **interest** the reader's and prompt them to keep reading. If the composition has a prompt, the introduction should **restate** or **summarize** some part of the prompt so that the reader will have an idea of what information will be in the essay. Finally, your introduction should include the **central idea**, the primary thing the essay will tell the reader.

> **Review Video: Introduction**
> Visit mometrix.com/academy and enter code: 961328

Body

In an essay's introduction, the writer states the central idea and prepares the reader for the information in the rest of the composition. In the body of the composition, the writer **explains**, **demonstrates**, and **gives more information about** the **central idea**. This is done using supporting details and examples that are relevant to the central idea of the composition. For example, if the composition's central idea is a vacation the writer took, the body will include descriptions of where the writer went, what they experienced, and what they thought of the trip. If the composition's central idea is the writer's opinion, the body will include examples and facts that show why he or she has formed that opinion. If composition's central idea is a topic and the writer wants to instruct the reader, the body will contain facts, explanations, and examples that help teach the reader about the central idea. A writer will use supporting details to explain the central idea throughout the body.

The body should also contain multiple paragraphs, and the order the writer puts these paragraphs in is important. Each paragraph should include at least one supporting detail, but a paragraph may include more than one if two or more supporting details work together to support the central idea. If the central idea is to describe something that happened, the paragraphs should match the order in which the events occurred. If the central idea is to present an opinion or instruct the reader, the paragraphs should be ordered in the way that would make the most sense to the reader. The order of body paragraphs is important because it can impact how easy a composition is to read.

> **Review Video: Drafting Body Paragraphs**
> Visit mometrix.com/academy and enter code: 724590

Choosing Supporting Details and Examples

When writing an informative or argumentative text, writers must choose supporting details carefully. Including details that are irrelevant, inaccurate, or vague does not strengthen the author's writing, while relevant, accurate, provable, and specific details do strengthen the author's writing. These details can make the writer's meaning clearer or give evidence that the author's points are true or logical. Such details may include examples or facts, such as statistics, statements from others who have authority on the subject, and common events or experiences. Choosing appropriate supporting details can also help the author show that they put effort into forming their ideas. This can also make the composition more intriguing and enjoyable to read, since the writer's own interest and insight will be apparent to the reader.

PARAGRAPHS

After the introduction of a passage, the body paragraphs will explain and elaborate upon the central idea. While each paragraph should relate to the central idea of the composition, each paragraph should focus on one point or supporting detail. Normally, a paragraph has a good topic sentence that summarizes the paragraph's main point. A topic sentence is a sentence that gives an introduction to the paragraph and its contents. Topic sentences should contain information that is more specific than what is in the introduction and may include a supporting detail, but they should not contain explanations or examples.

The next sentences in the paragraph should support the topic sentence. These sentences can contain examples, explanations, or other specific information that supports the topic sentence, which supports the central idea of the composition. While a paragraph may be structured in any way, as long as it logically provides information that supports the central idea, it can be best to use a template or pattern to make sure that each paragraph is complete and well organized. For example, a good template to follow is topic sentence, evidence, explanation, conclusion. This means that after the topic sentence, the next sentence should provide evidence, like a quote or example, that supports the paragraph's main point. Next, the paragraph should include a sentence that explains how that evidence supports the paragraph's main point. If there are multiple examples or quotes, more than one sentence may be used to explain them. Finally, there should be a concluding sentence that helps the reader understand the paragraph and prepares them for the next one.

A paragraph must contain enough information to support its main point and the composition's central idea. A paragraph of two or three sentences will most likely not support the main point or central idea because it is not likely to contain enough information, explanation, or evidence. When a paragraph does not support the main point or central idea, it does not help the writer achieve their purpose or goal for writing the essay. A helpful, informative paragraph will often have somewhere from three to five sentences. Also, it is important that the sentences within the paragraph lead the reader through the information. Each paragraph should flow logically and stay on topic throughout.

STARTING A NEW PARAGRAPH

For most forms of writing, you will need to use multiple paragraphs. This means that deciding when to start a new paragraph is very important. Reasons for starting a new paragraph include:

- To separate the introduction and conclusion from the body paragraphs
- To move from one supporting detail or point to another
- To indicate an important shift in time or place
- To show a comparison, contrast, or cause and effect relationship

TRANSITIONS

Transitions between sentences and paragraphs guide readers from idea to idea and show relationships between sentences and paragraphs. Writers should use transitions carefully and only when they are truly helpful. They should also be selected to fit the author's purpose. Transitions can show relationships such as time, comparison, an order of events, and cause and effect. Transitions are often used at the beginning of a phrase, sentence, or paragraph, since this helps prepare the reader for the next piece of information.

Review Video: Transitions in Writing
Visit mometrix.com/academy and enter code: 233246

Types of Transitional Words

Time	Afterward, immediately, earlier, meanwhile, recently, lately, now, since, soon, when, then, until, before, etc.
Sequence	too, first, second, further, moreover, also, again, and, next, still, besides, finally
Comparison	similarly, in the same way, likewise, also, again, once more
Contrasting	but, although, despite, however, instead, nevertheless, on the one hand... on the other hand, regardless, yet, in contrast
Cause and Effect	because, consequently, thus, therefore, then, to this end, since, so, as a result, if... then, accordingly
Examples	for example, for instance, such as, to illustrate, indeed, in fact, specifically
Place	near, far, here, there, to the left/right, next to, above, below, beyond, opposite, beside
Repetition, Summary, or Conclusion	as mentioned earlier, as noted, in other words, in short, on the whole, to summarize, therefore, as a result, to conclude, in conclusion
Addition	and, also, furthermore, moreover

Review Video: Transition Words
Visit mometrix.com/academy and enter code: 707563

Conclusion

The conclusion of a composition should summarize the central idea and show that it has been explained well. A good conclusion shows the reader why the author's central idea is meaningful and important and how the supporting details should help the reader understand the central idea. The conclusion should also give the reader something to think about that is related to the central idea. For example, in the conclusion, the author can invite readers to think about how they feel or what they think after reading the composition. Some things to avoid when writing conclusions include:

- Introducing a completely new idea
- Apologizing for one's opinions or writing
- Repeating the central idea word for word rather than summarizing them
- Using the conclusion to summarize every detail in the composition

Review Video: Drafting Conclusions
Visit mometrix.com/academy and enter code: 209408

Grammar

Subjects and Predicates

Subjects

Every sentence needs a subject and a predicate. The **subject** of a sentence names who or what the sentence is about. The subject may be directly stated in a sentence, or the subject may be implied. The **complete subject** includes the simple subject and any **modifiers**, such as adjectives, articles, prepositions, and adverbs, that go with it. To find the complete subject, ask *Who* or *What* before the verb to complete the question. The answer, including any modifiers, is the complete subject. To find the **simple subject**, remove all of the modifiers in the complete subject.

Examples:

simple subject: car

The small, red car is the one that he wants for Christmas.

complete subject: The small, red car

simple subject: artist

The young artist is coming over for dinner.

complete subject: The young artist

Review Video: Subjects in English
Visit mometrix.com/academy and enter code: 444771

An imperative sentence is a sentence that gives someone instructions or makes a request to someone. In **imperative** sentences, the verb's subject is understood, but is not actually present in the sentence. For example, this about the sentence *Drive to the store*. This sentence is a command, and the subject is *you*. If the subject were directly stated, the sentence would be *You, drive to the store*. Another fact to consider is that, normally, the subject comes before the verb. However, the subject comes after the verb in sentences that begin with *There are* or *There was*.

Direct:

John knows the way to the park.	Who knows the way to the park?	John
The cookies need ten more minutes.	What needs ten minutes?	The cookies
By five o'clock, Bill will need to leave.	Who needs to leave?	Bill
There are five letters on the table for him.	What is on the table?	Five letters
There were coffee and doughnuts in the house.	What was in the house?	Coffee and doughnuts

Implied:

Go to the post office for me.	Who is going to the post office?	You
Come and sit with me, please?	Who needs to come and sit?	You

Predicates

In a sentence, there is always a predicate and a subject. The subject tells what the sentence is about, and the **predicate** explains or describes the subject.

Think about the sentence *He sings*. In this sentence, we have a subject, *He*, and a predicate, *sings*. This is all that is needed for a sentence to be complete. Most sentences contain more information, but if this is all the information that is given in a sentence, then it is a complete sentence.

Now, let's look at another sentence: *John and Jane sing on Tuesday nights at the dance hall.*

subject: John and Jane | predicate: sing on Tuesday nights at the dance hall.

John and Jane sing on Tuesday nights at the dance hall.

Subject-Verb Agreement

Verbs **agree** with their subjects in number. In other words, singular subjects need singular verbs. Plural subjects need plural verbs. **Singular** is for **one** person, place, or thing. **Plural** is for **more than one** person, place, or thing. Subjects and verbs must also share the same point of view, as in first, second, or third person.

Review Video: Subject-Verb Agreement
Visit mometrix.com/academy and enter code: 479190

Number Agreement Examples:

singular subject: Dan | singular verb: calls

Single Subject and Verb: Dan calls home.

Dan is one person. So, the singular verb *calls* is needed.

plural subject: Dan and Bob | plural verb: call

Plural Subject and Verb: Dan and Bob call home.

More than one person needs the plural verb *call.*

Person Agreement Examples:

First Person: I *am* walking.

Second Person: You *are* walking.

Third Person: He *is* walking.

Complications with Subject-Verb Agreement

Words Between Subject and Verb

Words that come between the simple subject and the verb do not affect subject-verb agreement.

Examples:

singular subject: joy | singular verb: returns

The joy of my life returns home tonight.

The phrase *of my life* does not affect the verb *returns.*

singular subject / singular verb

The question that still remains unanswered is "Who are you?"

Don't let the phrase "*that still remains…*" confuse you. The subject *question* goes with the verb *is*.

Compound Subjects

A compound subject is formed when two or more nouns joined by *and*, *or*, or *nor* act together as the subject of the sentence.

Joined by And

When a compound subject is joined by *and*, it is treated as a plural subject and requires a plural verb.

Examples:

plural subject / plural verb

You and Jon are invited to come to my house.

plural subject / plural verb

The pencil and paper belong to me.

Joined by Or/Nor

For a compound subject joined by *or* or *nor*, the verb must agree in number with the part of the subject that is closest to the verb.

Examples:

subject / verb

Today or tomorrow is the day.

subject / verb

Stan or Phil wants to read the book.

subject / verb

Neither the pen nor the book is on the desk.

subject / verb

Either the blanket or pillows arrive this afternoon.

Indefinite Pronouns as Subject

An indefinite pronoun is a pronoun that does not refer to a specific noun. Different indefinite pronouns are used as a singular noun, a plural noun, or change depending on how they are used.

Always Singular

Pronouns such as *each*, *either*, *everybody*, *anybody*, *somebody*, and *nobody* are always singular. This is because these pronouns always stand in for one person, place, or thing.

Examples:

singular subject: Each / singular verb: has

Each of the runners has a different bib number.

singular verb: Is / singular subject: either

Is either of you ready for the game?

Note: The words *each* and *either* can also be used as adjectives. For example, *each* person is unique. When one of these adjectives modifies the subject of a sentence, it is always a singular subject.

singular subject: Everybody / singular verb: grows

Everybody grows a day older every day.

singular subject: Anybody / singular verb: is

Anybody is welcome to bring a tent.

ALWAYS PLURAL

Pronouns such as *both*, *several*, and *many* are always plural. This is because these pronouns always stand in for more than one person, place, thing, or idea.

Examples:

plural subject: Both / plural verb: were

Both of the siblings were too tired to argue.

plural subject: Many / plural verb: have tried

Many have tried, but none have succeeded.

DEPEND ON CONTEXT

Pronouns such as *some*, *any*, *all*, *none*, *more*, and *most* can be either singular or plural depending on what they are representing in the context of the sentence.

Examples:

singular subject: All / singular verb: was

All of my dog's food was still there in his bowl.

plural subject: all / plural verb: were

By the end of the night, all of my guests were already excited about coming to my next party.

OTHER CASES INVOLVING PLURAL OR IRREGULAR FORM

Some nouns are **singular in meaning but plural in form**: news, mathematics, physics, and economics.

The *news is* coming on now.

Mathematics is my favorite class.

Some nouns are plural in form and meaning, and have **no singular equivalent**: scissors and pants.

Do these *pants come* with a shirt?

The *scissors are* for my project.

Note: Look to your **dictionary** for help when you aren't sure whether a noun with a plural form has a singular or plural meaning.

EXAMPLE

Which word should go in the blank?

If Kelly is going to the party, Joan and Susan ____ going to the store.

a. Is
b. Are
c. Am
d. Was

Try using each choice in the sentence. Choice A, *is*, forms this sentence: If Kelly is going to the party, Joan and Susan is going to the store. There are two people, Joan and Susan, who are going to the store. This makes the subject of the clause plural. *Is* is a singular verb, meaning it does not agree with the subject and cannot be the answer.

Choice B, *are*, forms this sentence: If Kelly is going to the party, Joan and Susan are going to the store. The subject of the clause is still plural. But *are* is a plural verb! The subject and verb agree, so *are* is the correct answer.

Choice C, *am*, forms this sentence: If Kelly is going to the party, Joan and Susan am going to the store. *Am* is a singular verb, and it is also only used in first person, when the writer or speaker is referring to themself. The subject of the clause is plural, and the sentence is in third person, so *am* is not the correct answer.

Choice D, *was*, forms this sentence: If Kelly is going to the party, Joan and Susan was going to the store. *Was* is a singular verb, so it does not agree with the plural subject in this clause.

COMPLEMENTS

A complement is a noun, pronoun, or adjective that is used to give more information about the subject or verb in the sentence.

DIRECT OBJECTS

A direct object is a noun or pronoun that takes or receives the **action** of a verb. A complete sentence does not need a direct object, so not all sentences will have them. When you are looking for a direct object, find the verb and ask *who* or *what.*

Examples:

I took *the blanket.*

Jane read *books.*

INDIRECT OBJECTS

An indirect object is a word or group of words that show how an action had an **influence** on someone or something. If there is an indirect object in a sentence, then you always have a direct object in the sentence. When you are looking for the indirect object, find the verb and ask *to*, *for*, *whom*, or *what*.

Examples:

We taught the old dog (indirect object) a new trick (direct object).

I gave them (indirect object) a math lesson (direct object).

Review Video: Direct and Indirect Objects
Visit mometrix.com/academy and enter code: 817385

Pronoun-Antecedent Agreement

The **antecedent** is the noun that has been replaced by a pronoun. A pronoun and its antecedent **agree** when they have the same number (singular or plural) and gender (male, female, or neutral).

Examples:

Singular agreement: John (antecedent) came into town, and he (pronoun) played for us.

Plural agreement: John and Rick (antecedent) came into town, and they (pronoun) played for us.

To determine which is the correct pronoun to use in a compound subject or object, try each pronoun **alone** in place of the compound in the sentence. Your knowledge of pronouns will tell you which one is correct.

Example:

Bob and (I, me) will be going.

Test: (1) *I will be going* or (2) *Me will be going*. The second choice cannot be correct because *me* cannot be used as the subject of a sentence. Instead, *me* is used as an object.

Answer: Bob and I will be going.

When a pronoun is used with a noun immediately following (as in "we boys"), try the sentence **without the added noun**.

Example:

(We/Us) boys played football last year.

Test: (1) *We played football last yea*r or (2) *Us played football last year*. Again, the second choice cannot be correct because *us* cannot be used as a subject of a sentence. Instead, *us* is used as an object.

Answer: We boys played football last year.

Review Video: Pronoun Usage
Visit mometrix.com/academy and enter code: 666500

Review Video: Pronoun-Antecedent Agreement
Visit mometrix.com/academy and enter code: 919704

A pronoun should point clearly to the **antecedent**. Here is how a pronoun reference can be unhelpful if it is puzzling or not directly stated.

Unhelpful: Ron and Jim (antecedent) went to the store, and he (pronoun) bought soda.

Who bought soda? Ron or Jim?

Helpful: Jim (antecedent) went to the store, and he (pronoun) bought soda.

The sentence is clear. Jim bought the soda.

Example

Tom printed his ticket to the concert, but he forgot ____ at home.

Which pronoun should go in the blank?

a. It
b. Them
c. Him
d. He

What is the antecedent that the missing pronoun must match? There are only four nouns in the sentence. They are *Tom*, *ticket*, *concert*, and *home*. Which one should the missing pronoun refer to? Tom is the one who forgot something, so the pronoun does not refer to Tom. The concert is not at Tom's home, so he cannot forget the concert at home. It is also not logical to say that Tom forgot his home at home The antecedent must be *ticket*.

Choice A says that the missing pronoun is *it*. The pronoun refers to *ticket*, which is a singular noun. A ticket is also a nonliving thing. The missing pronoun is also the object in the second clause. *It* is singular, refers to nonliving nouns, and can be used as the object. Choice A is correct.

Choice B says that the missing pronoun is *them*. The pronoun refers to the singular noun *ticket*. While *them* can be used to refer to nonliving nouns and can be the object of a sentence, it is a plural pronoun. Choice B is incorrect.

Choice C says that the missing pronoun is *him*. The missing pronoun refers to a nonliving thing, not a human. *Him* is an objective personal pronoun and is singular, but it only refers to living nouns. *Him* cannot represent *ticket*, so choice C is incorrect.

Choice D says that the missing pronoun is *he*. The missing pronoun refers to a nonliving noun and is the object of the second sentence. While *he* is a singular pronoun, it can only be used as the subject of a sentence and only refers to living nouns. Choice D is incorrect.

PHRASES

A phrase is a group of words that functions as a single part of speech, usually a noun, adjective, or adverb. A **phrase** is not a complete thought, and does not contain a subject, but it adds detail or explanation to a sentence, or renames something within the sentence.

CLAUSES

A clause is a group of words that contains both a subject and a predicate (verb). There are two types of clauses: independent and dependent. An **independent clause** contains a complete thought, while a **dependent (or subordinate) clause** does not. A dependent clause includes a subject and a verb, and may also contain additional information, but it cannot stand as a complete thought without being joined to an independent clause. Dependent clauses function within sentences as adjectives, adverbs, or nouns.

Example:

independent clause: I am running | dependent clause: because I want to stay in shape.

I am running because I want to stay in shape.

The clause *I am running* is an independent clause: it has a subject and a verb, and it gives a complete thought. The clause *because I want to stay in shape* is a dependent clause: it has a subject and a verb, but it does not express a complete thought. This is due to the fact that it begins with *because*, which shows that there is more information needed to complete the thought. This dependent clause adds detail to the independent clause to which it is attached.

> **Review Video: Independent and Dependent Clauses**
> Visit mometrix.com/academy and enter code: 556903

SENTENCE STRUCTURE

Sentence structure is based on the type and number of clauses in the sentence. Two common sentence structures are simple sentences and compound sentences:

Simple: A simple sentence has one independent clause with no dependent clauses. A simple sentence may have a **compound subject** or a **compound verb**, or both.

Examples:

single subject | single verb
Judy watered the lawn.

compound subject | single verb
Judy and Alan watered the lawn.

single subject | compound verb | compound verb
Judy watered the lawn and pulled weeds.

compound subject | compound verb | compound verb
Judy and Alan watered the lawn and pulled weeds.

Compound: A compound sentence has two or more independent clauses with no dependent clauses. Usually, the independent clauses are joined with a comma and a coordinating conjunction or with a semicolon.

Examples:

independent clause | independent clause
The time has come, and we are ready.

independent clause | independent clause
I woke up at dawn; the sun was just coming up.

Complex: A complex sentence has one independent clause and at least one dependent clause.

Examples:

dependent clause | independent clause
Although he had the flu, Harry went to work.

independent clause | dependent clause
Marcia got married after she finished college.

Review Video: Sentence Structure
Visit mometrix.com/academy and enter code: 700478

SENTENCE FRAGMENTS

Recall that a group of words must contain at least one **independent clause** in order to be considered a sentence. If it doesn't contain even one independent clause, it is called a **sentence fragment**.

Choosing the best steps for **repairing** a sentence fragment depends on what type of fragment it is. If the fragment is a dependent clause, it can sometimes be fixed by simply removing a subordinating word, such as *when*, *because*, or *if*, from the beginning of the fragment. Alternatively, a dependent clause can be joined to a closely related neighboring sentence. If the fragment is missing some required part, like a subject or a verb, it may be fixed by simply adding the missing part.

Examples:

Fragment: Because he wanted to sail the Mediterranean.

Removed subordinating word: He wanted to sail the Mediterranean.

Combined with another sentence: Because he wanted to sail the Mediterranean, he booked a Greek island cruise.

Example

Which of the following changes will NOT correct this sentence fragment?

Although she had found the coin first.

a. Remove *Although.*
b. Add a comma and *she let her brother keep it* after *first.*
c. Add *She let her brother keep the coin* before *although.*
d. Remove *first.*

Choice A suggests removing the word *although* to form the following sentence: She found the coin first. This option removes the subordinating conjunction to make the clause independent. The resulting sentence is complete, so removing *although* is an acceptable way to correct the fragment. Choice A is incorrect.

Choice B forms the following sentence: Although she had found the coin first, she let her brother keep it. A comma and an independent clause have been added to the sentence fragment to form a complex sentence. The resulting sentence is complete and written correctly, so choice B is incorrect.

Choice C forms the following sentence: She let her brother keep the coin although she had found the coin first. An independent clause has been added before the sentence fragment to form a complex sentence. This sentence is correctly written and complete, so choice C is an acceptable way to correct the fragment. Choice C is incorrect.

Choice D removes the word *first*, leaving *Although she had found the coin*. This is still a sentence fragment, since it is a single dependent clause. Choice D does not correct the fragment, so D is correct.

Run-on Sentences

Run-on sentences consist of multiple independent clauses that have not been joined together properly. Run-on sentences can be corrected in several different ways:

Join clauses properly: This can be done with a comma and coordinating conjunction, with a semicolon, or with a colon or dash if the second clause is explaining something in the first clause.

Example:

Incorrect: I went on the trip, we visited lots of castles.

Corrected: I went on the trip, and we visited lots of castles.

Split into separate sentences: This correction is best to use when the independent clauses are very long or when they are not closely related.

Example:

> **Incorrect**: The drive to New York takes ten hours, my uncle lives in Boston.
>
> **Corrected**: The drive to New York takes ten hours. My uncle lives in Boston.

Make one clause dependent: This is the easiest way to make the sentence correct and more interesting at the same time. It's often as simple as adding a subordinating word between the two clauses or before the first clause.

Example:

> **Incorrect**: I finally made it to the store and I bought some eggs.
>
> **Corrected**: When I finally made it to the store, I bought some eggs.

Reduce to one clause with a compound verb: If both clauses have the same subject, remove the subject from the second clause, and you now have just one clause with a compound verb.

Example:

> **Incorrect**: The drive to New York takes ten hours, it makes me very tired.
>
> **Corrected**: The drive to New York takes ten hours and makes me very tired.

Note: While these are the simplest ways to correct a run-on sentence, often the best way is to completely reorganize the thoughts in the sentence and rewrite it.

Comma Splices

A comma splice is a specific error that may appear in a run-on sentence. When a sentence has two independent clauses, but the clauses are joined with only a comma, a **comma splice** is formed. Remember that if two independent clauses are joined with a comma, a coordinating conjunction is also needed. Most of the solutions for fixing run-on sentences can also be used to correct a comma splice.

Review Video: Fragments and Run-on Sentences
Visit mometrix.com/academy and enter code: 541989

Example

Rick wants to go see a movie tomorrow he would miss his sister's recital.

Identify the change that would NOT correct this run-on sentence.

a. Add a comma after *tomorrow*.
b. Split it into two sentences between *tomorrow* and *he*.
c. Add a comma and *but* after *tomorrow*.
d. Add a subordinating conjunction to make one of the clauses dependent.

Choice A says to add a comma after *tomorrow*. This forms the following sentence: Rick wants to go see a movie tomorrow, he would miss his sister's recital. A comma has been used to join two independent clauses, but there is no coordinating conjunction. This choice forms a comma splice, so it is not an acceptable correction for this sentence. Choice A is the correct answer.

Choice B says to split the sentence into two sentences. This forms the following two sentences: Rick wants to go see a movie tomorrow. He would miss his sister's recital. Both of these sentences are complete. This is an acceptable way to correct the run-on sentence, so choice B is incorrect.

Choice C says to add a coordinating conjunction after *tomorrow*. This forms the following sentence: Rick wants to go see a movie tomorrow, but he would miss his sister's recital. A comma and a coordinating conjunction have been added between the two independent clauses. This is an acceptable way to correct a run-on sentence. Choice C is incorrect.

Choice D says to add a subordinating conjunction to make one of the sentences dependent. There are many new sentences that could be created by adding a subordinating conjunction. For example, consider the following sentence: Although Rick wants to go see a movie tomorrow, he would miss his sister's recital. Alternatively, the following sentence could also be created: Rick wants to go see a movie tomorrow even though he would miss his sister's recital. Both of these sentences have an independent clause and a dependent clause. These sentences are both complete and written correctly, so choice D is incorrect.

Example

Identify the sentence that has a comma splice.

a. Tom stopped at the store to buy supplies and his family met him at the campsite.
b. The ball rolled into the living room quietly, but it still startled the dog.
c. Theresa brought her mom some flowers, her mom did not have a vase.
d. Sweet potatoes, pecans, and brown sugar are all ingredients in my cousin's sweet potato casserole.

Choice A has two independent clauses joined by a coordinating conjunction. This is incorrect because there should be a comma before the coordinating conjunction. While the sentence is written incorrectly, there is no comma, so this sentence does not have a comma splice. Choice A is incorrect.

Choice B has two independent clauses joined by a comma and a coordinating conjunction. This is the correct way to write a compound sentence, so there is no error here. Choice B is incorrect.

Choice C has two independent clauses joined by a comma. This is incorrect because independent clauses should be joined together by a comma and a coordinating conjunction. When the comma is present without a coordinating conjunction between two independent clauses, a comma splice is formed. This means that choice C is correct.

Choice D is a simple sentence that contains one independent clause. The only commas used in this sentence are used to separate items in a list. There are no clauses that need to be joined or errors related to commas, so choice D does not contain a comma splice. Choice D is incorrect.

The Eight Parts of Speech

Nouns

When you talk about a person, place, thing, or idea, you are talking about a **noun**. The two main types of nouns are **common** and **proper** nouns.

Common Nouns

Common nouns are generic names for people, places, and things. Common nouns are not usually capitalized.

Examples of common nouns:

People: boy, girl, worker, manager

Places: school, bank, library, home

Things: dog, cat, truck, car

Proper Nouns

Proper nouns name specific people, places, or things. All proper nouns are capitalized.

Examples of proper nouns:

People: Abraham Lincoln, George Washington, Martin Luther King, Jr.

Places: Los Angeles, California; New York; Asia

Things: Statue of Liberty, Earth, Lincoln Memorial

Note: When referring to the planet that we live on, capitalize *Earth*. When referring to the dirt, rocks, or land, lowercase *earth*.

Singular and Plural Nouns

Singular nouns name **one** person, place, thing, or idea. **Plural nouns** name **more than one** person, place, thing, or idea. Most nouns have both a singular and plural form. Many plural nouns are spelled like the singular noun with an *-s* at the end, but this is not true for all plural nouns. Singular nouns that already end in an *s*, *o*, *ch*, *sh*, or *x* usually end in *-es* when they are in the plural form. Singular nouns that end in a consonant followed by the letter *y* will usually lose the *y* and end in *-ies* in the plural form, and words that end with the letter *f* or *fe* will usually lose the *f* and end in *-ves*.

Some plural nouns have much different spellings than their singular form, and some plural nouns are spelled the same as their singular form. There are more rules for spelling plural nouns, but these are the most common spelling changes.

Examples of singular nouns:

Typical nouns: dog, pencil, girl, store, hope, stingray

Nouns ending in *s*, *o*, *ch*, *sh*, or *x*: mass, hero, lunch, polish, fox

Nouns ending in a consonant and *y*: puppy, baby, fairy, sky

Nouns ending in *f* or *fe*: self, life, calf, hoof

Examples of plural nouns:

Typical nouns: dogs, pencils, girls, stores, hopes, stingrays

Nouns ending in *s*, *o*, *ch*, *sh*, or *x*: masses, heroes, lunches, polishes, foxes

Nouns ending in a consonant and *y*: puppies, babies, fairies, skies

Nouns ending in a vowel and *f* or *fe*: selves, lives, calves, hooves

Collective Nouns

Collective nouns are the names for a group of people, places, or things that function like singular nouns. The following are examples of collective nouns: *class, company, dozen, group, herd, team,* and *public*. Collective nouns usually require an article, such as *a*, *an*, and *the*, which shows that the noun is a single unit. For example, a choir is a group of singers. Even though there are many singers in a choir, the word choir describes a single group. If we refer to the members of the group, and not the group itself, it is no longer a collective noun.

Incorrect: The *choir are* going to compete nationally this year.

Correct: The *choir is* going to compete nationally this year.

Incorrect: The *members* of the choir *is* competing nationally this year.

Correct: The *members* of the choir *are* competing nationally this year.

Pronouns

Pronouns are words that are used to stand in for nouns. There are several different types of pronouns, but the two main types are subjective and objective pronouns. **Subjective** nouns and pronouns that those that are the subject of a sentence. **Objective** nouns and pronouns are those that are an object in a sentence. Another important type of pronoun is the personal pronoun, which refers to people. Personal pronouns can be subjective or objective. **Possessive** nouns and pronouns show possession or ownership. Pronouns can also be singular or plural.

Singular

Subjective	Objective	Possessive
I	Me	My, Mine
You	You	Your, Yours
He	Him	His
She	Her	Her, hers
It	It	Its
Who	Whom	Whose

Plural

Subjective	Objective	Possessive
we	us	our, ours
you	you	your, yours
they	them	their, theirs

Reflexive: Reflexive pronouns are pronouns that function as the object of a sentence and refer to the subject. Examples of reflexive pronouns include *myself, yourself, himself, herself, itself, ourselves, yourselves*, and *themselves*.

Indefinite: Indefinite pronouns are used to refer to multiple nouns or an undefined noun. Examples of indefinite nouns include *all, any, each, everyone, either/neither, one, some*, and *several*.

Relative: Relative pronouns are used to connect relative clauses that specify or describe a noun to the rest of the sentence. Examples of relative pronouns include *which*, *who*, *whom*, and *whose*.

Review Video: Nouns and Pronouns
Visit mometrix.com/academy and enter code: 312073

VERBS

If you want to write a sentence, then you need a verb. Without a verb, you have no sentence. The verb of a sentence indicates action or being. In other words, the verb shows something's action or state of being or the action that has been done to something.

TRANSITIVE AND INTRANSITIVE VERBS

A **transitive verb** is a verb whose action (e.g., drive, run, jump) indicates a receiver (e.g., car, dog, kangaroo). **Intransitive verbs** do not indicate a receiver of an action. In other words, the action of the verb does not point to a subject or object.

Transitive: He plays the piano. | The piano was played by him.

Intransitive: He plays. | John plays well.

ACTION VERBS AND LINKING VERBS

Action verbs show what the subject is doing. In other words, an action verb shows action. **Linking verbs** link the subject of a sentence to a noun or pronoun. They can also link a subject to an adjective, so the linking verb helps create a description. You always need a verb if you want a complete sentence. However, linking verbs on their own cannot be a complete sentence. Any verb that shows a condition and connects to a noun, pronoun, or adjective that describes the subject of a sentence is a linking verb.

Action: He sings. | Run! | Go! | I talk with him every day. | She reads.

Linking:

Incorrect: I am.

Correct: I am John. | I smell roses. | I feel tired.

Review Video: Action Verbs and Linking Verbs
Visit mometrix.com/academy and enter code: 743142

VOICE

Transitive verbs come in active or passive **voice**. If something does an action or is acted upon, then you will know whether a verb is active or passive. When the subject of the sentence is doing the action, the verb is in **active voice**. When the subject is acted upon, the verb is in **passive voice**.

Active: Jon drew the picture. (The subject *Jon* is doing the action of *drawing a picture*.)

Passive: The picture is drawn by Jon. (The subject *picture* is receiving the action from Jon.)

Example

Which of the following sentences is written in passive voice?

a. The alligator quickly swam through the swamp.
b. She dug up the hidden treasure.
c. The vase was painted by an artist.
d. The bag held many apples.

In choice A, the subject is *alligator*, the verb is *swam*, and the object is *swamp*. Did the subject or the object do the action in this sentence? The alligator swam and acted upon the swamp. The subject did the action, so choice A is in active voice.

In choice B, the subject is *she*, the verb is *dug*, and the object is *hidden treasure*. Did the subject or the object do the action? She dug and acted upon the hidden treasure. The subject did the action, so choice B is in active voice.

In choice C, the subject is *vase*, the verb is *was painted*, and the object is *artist*. Did the subject or the object do the action? The vase simply existed. The painter painted and acted upon the vase. The object did the action, so choice C is in passive voice. Choice C is correct.

In choice D, the subject is *bag*, the verb is *held*, and the object is *apples*. Did the subject or the object do the action? The bag held and acted upon the apples. The subject did the action, so choice D is in active voice.

Verb Tenses

A verb **tense** shows the different form of a verb to point to the time of an action. The present and past tense are indicated by the verb's form. An action in the present, *I talk,* can change form for the past: *I talked*. However, for future tense, an auxiliary, or helping, verb is sometimes needed to show the change in form. When writing a composition, it is important to use verb tenses consistently. Choose the best tense for the composition and do not switch to a different tense unless it is necessary or appropriate for a particular sentence or paragraph.

Present: I talk
Past: I talked
Future: I will talk

Present: The action happens at the current time.

Example: He *walks* to the store every morning.

Past: The action happened in the past.

Example: He *walked* to the store an hour ago.

Future: The action is going to happen later.

Example: I *will walk* to the store tomorrow.

Review Video: Verb Tenses
Visit mometrix.com/academy and enter code: 269472

Irregular Verbs

While most verbs gain the suffix -ed when used in the past tense, irregular verbs receive different spelling changes when they are written in the past tense. For example, *walk* is a regular verb, and it becomes *walked* when written in the past tense. However, *run* is an irregular verb because it becomes *ran* when written in the past tense.

Example

> My mother _____ me about the big nest of ants near the sandbox. I thanked her for telling me!

Which of the following verbs should go in the blank?

a. Warn
b. Warned
c. Will warn
d. Warns

First, look at the sentences. The first sentence does not have enough information to show which tense it is in. However, the second sentence says that the child thanked the mother. The verb here is *thanked*, which is the past-tense form of *thank*. Because the second sentence is in the past tense, it makes sense to say that the first sentence is also in past tense.

Choice A says that the missing verb is *warn*. *Warn* is a present-tense verb, but it can be used in the future tense if a helping verb is present. However, this sentence is in past tense, so it needs a past-tense verb. Choice A is wrong.

Choice B says that the missing verb is *warned*. *Warned* is a past-tense verb, and it logically completes the sentence. Choice B is correct!

Choice C says that the missing verb is *will warn*. *Will warn* is a future-tense verb, meaning that it describes an action that will occur in the future. However, since the speaker already thanked his or her mother for the warning, it is not logical to use a future-tense verb in the blank. Choice C is incorrect.

Choice D says that the missing verb is *warns*. *Warn* is usually used with plural subjects, and *warns* used with single subjects. *Warns* can be used in the future or present tense, but it cannot be used in the past tense. Since the sentence is in the past tense, it needs a past-tense verb, so D is incorrect.

Adjectives

An **adjective** is a word that is used to modify a noun or pronoun. An adjective answers a question: *Which one? What kind?* or *How many?* Usually, adjectives come before the words that they modify, but they may also come after a linking verb.

> Which one? The *third* suit is my favorite.
>
> What kind? This suit is *navy blue*.
>
> How many? I am going to buy *four* pairs of socks to match the suit.

Review Video: Descriptive Text Visit mometrix.com/academy and enter code: 174903

Comparison with Adjectives

Some adjectives are relative, and other adjectives are absolute. Adjectives that are **relative** can show the comparison between things. **Absolute** adjectives can also show comparison, but they do so in a different way. Let's say that you are reading two books. You think that one book is perfect, and the other book is not exactly perfect. It is not possible for one book to be more perfect than the other. Either you think that the book is perfect, or you think that the book is imperfect. In this case, perfect and imperfect are absolute adjectives.

Relative adjectives will show the different **degrees** of something or someone to something else or someone else. The three degrees of adjectives include positive, comparative, and superlative.

The **positive** degree is the normal form of an adjective.

> Example: This work is *difficult.* | She is *smart.*

The **comparative** degree compares one person or thing to another person or thing.

> Example: This work is *more difficult* than your work. | She is *smarter* than me.

The **superlative** degree compares more than two people or things.

> Example: This is the *most difficult* work of my life. | She is the *smartest* lady in school.

Review Video: Adjectives
Visit mometrix.com/academy and enter code: 470154

Adverbs

An **adverb** is a word that is used to **modify,** or describe, a verb, adjective, or another adverb. Usually, adverbs answer one of these questions: *When? Where? How?* and *Why?* The negatives *not* and *never* are considered adverbs. Adverbs that modify adjectives or other adverbs **strengthen** or **weaken** the words that they modify.

Examples:

> He walks *quickly* through the crowd.
>
> The water flows *smoothly* on the rocks.

Note: Adverbs are usually indicated by the suffix *-ly*, which has been added to the root word. For instance, *quick* can be made into an adverb by adding *-ly* to construct *quickly*. Some words that end in *-ly* do not follow this rule and can function as other parts of speech. Examples of adjectives ending in *-ly* include: *early, friendly, holy, lonely, silly*, and *ugly*. To know if a word that ends in *-ly* is an adjective or adverb, check your dictionary. Also, while many adverbs end in *-ly*, you need to remember that not all adverbs end in *-ly*.

Examples:

> He is *never* angry.
>
> You are *too* irresponsible to travel alone.

TYPES OF ADVERBS

Different types of adverbs are used to describe particular aspects of a verb, adjective, or other adverb. The following are examples of common types of adverbs:

Time: Some adverbs show when something was done, such as *yesterday*, *today*, or *in two days*.

Manner: Some adverbs show the way something was done, such as *hurriedly*, *neatly*, *grumpily*, or *loudly*.

Frequency: Some adverbs show how often something was done, such as *seldom*, *often*, *never*, or *often*.

Degree: Some adverbs show how much or to what degree something was done, such as *completely*, *barely*, *highly*, or *halfway*.

Conjunctive: Conjunctive adverbs are used similarly to conjunctions, as they connect different ideas, but they can connect ideas from different clauses or sentences. Some examples of conjunctive adverbs are *however*, *alternatively*, *likewise*, and *then*.

COMPARISON WITH ADVERBS

The rules for comparing adverbs are the same as the rules for adjectives.

The **positive** degree is the standard form of an adverb.

> Example: He arrives *soon*. | She speaks *softly* to her friends.

The **comparative** degree compares one person or thing to another person or thing.

> Example: He arrives *sooner* than Sarah. | She speaks *more softly* than him.

The **superlative** degree compares more than two people or things.

> Example: He arrives *soonest* of the group. | She speaks the *most softly* of any of her friends.

Review Video: Adverbs
Visit mometrix.com/academy and enter code: 713951

PREPOSITIONS

A **preposition** is a word placed before a noun or pronoun that shows the relationship between an object and another word in the sentence.

Common prepositions:

about	before	during	on	under
after	beneath	for	over	until
against	between	from	past	up
among	beyond	in	through	with
around	by	of	to	within
at	down	off	toward	without

Examples:

The napkin is *in* the drawer.

The Earth rotates *around* the Sun.

The needle is *beneath* the haystack.

Can you find "me" *among* the words?

Prepositional Phrases

One important thing to know about prepositions is that they form special phrases, called prepositional phrases. A **prepositional phrase** begins with a preposition and ends with a noun or pronoun that is the object of the preposition. Normally, the prepositional phrase functions as an **adjective** or an **adverb** within the sentence.

Examples:

The picnic is [on the blanket]^(prepositional phrase).

I am sick [with a fever]^(prepositional phrase) today.

[Among the many flowers,]^(prepositional phrase) John found a four-leaf clover.

Be careful not to mistake the object in a prepositional phrase as the subject of a sentence. The subject of the sentence will not be found in a prepositional phrase because a prepositional phrase is used to describe how an object is related to the subject. Prepositional phrases do not influence subject-verb agreement.

Review Video: Prepositions
Visit mometrix.com/academy and enter code: 946763

Example

Which of the following could NOT complete the sentence?

She went ____ the cave.

a. Sadly
b. Into
c. From
d. Through

Choice A says that the missing word is *sadly*. The blank is between *went* and *the cave*, meaning that the missing word will connect these pieces of the sentence. While *sadly* could be used here to show how the girl felt, there would still be missing information. A preposition is needed here to show whether she entered, exited, or stood outside of the cave. *Sadly* is an adverb, so A is the correct answer.

Choice B says that *into* would complete the sentence. Does *into* complete the sentence without leaving missing information? To say *she went into the cave* is a logical, complete sentence. Choice B is incorrect.

Choice C says that the missing word is *from*. This creates the sentence *she went from the cave*. Since she could have left the cave to go somewhere else, this is also a logical, complete sentence. Choice C is incorrect.

Choice D says that *through* would complete the sentence. The sentence would read *she went through the cave*. Since she could have explored the whole cave or found an exit on the other side of it, *through* can logically complete the sentence. Choice D is incorrect.

EXAMPLE

Identify the prepositional phrase in the following sentence.

Mable visited the store to buy some vegetables.

a. To buy
b. Visited the store
c. The store to buy
d. To buy some vegetables

Remember the pieces of a prepositional phrase. Prepositional phrases should begin with a preposition and end with a noun or pronoun. Considering these rules, can any of the answer choices be eliminated? Choice B and choice C can be eliminated because neither choice begins with a preposition!

That leaves choices A and D. Choice A says that the prepositional phrase is *to buy*. This does start with a preposition, and it does give more information about Mable's trip to the store. However, it does not end with a noun or pronoun. Choice D says that the prepositional phrase is *to buy some vegetables*. Choice D begins with a preposition and ends with a noun, and it explains why Mabel went to the store.

Choice D is the only choice that has all of the pieces of a prepositional phrase, so D is correct!

EXAMPLE

A band with 15 members _____ performing at my restaurant tonight.

Identify the verb that best completes the sentence.

a. Were
b. Is
c. Are
d. Are not

This question is asking which verb should go in the blank. There are a couple of reasons why choosing the correct verb for this sentence may be confusing. First of all, there are two nouns that appear before the verb. Second, one of these nouns is singular and one is plural.

The first step is to determine which noun goes with the verb. The two nouns are *band* and *members*. While *members* is closest to the blank, it is part of a prepositional phrase that describes *band*. The subject of the sentence is *band*, so the verb must agree with *band*.

Is *band* singular or plural? The sentence says that the band has multiple members, but there is only one band. *Band* is a collective noun, meaning that it is a singular noun. This means that the correct verb will also be singular. With this in mind, can any of the answer choices be eliminated?

Choices A, C, and D are all plural verbs. Even though the blank appears after a plural noun, this noun is part of a prepositional phrase. The verb should match the singular subject *band*. The only choice with a singular verb is choice B, so B is the correct answer.

CONJUNCTIONS

Conjunctions join words, phrases, or clauses and they show the connection between the joined pieces. **Coordinating conjunctions** connect equal parts of sentences. Coordinating conjunctions can also be used to create compound subjects and compound predicates, in addition to compound sentences.

COORDINATING CONJUNCTIONS

The **coordinating conjunctions** include: *and, but, yet, or, nor, for,* and *so*

Compound Subjects:

compound subject

Terry *and* Marissa went to the movies last Saturday.

compund subject

Either pumpkin pie *or* apple pie would be a good dessert to bring to Thanksgiving dinner.

compound subject

Neither the clownfish *nor* the goldfish liked the new fish food very much.

Compound Predicates:

compound predicate

Veronica left school *and* picked up her sister from soccer practice.

compound predicate

The cat did not take a nap *or* play with the dog yesterday.

Compound Sentences:

The rock was small, *but* it was heavy.

She drove in the night, *and* he drove in the day.

Bill dressed nicely today, *for* he must give an important presentation this afternoon.

Correlative Conjunctions

Some examples of **correlative conjunctions** are: *either...or* | *neither...nor* | *not only...but also*. When one correlative conjunction is used, its matching correlative conjunction will be used later in the sentence.

Examples:

> *Either* you are coming *or* you are staying.
>
> He *not only* ran three miles *but also* swam 200 yards.

Review Video: Coordinating and Correlative Conjunctions
Visit mometrix.com/academy and enter code: 390329

Subordinating Conjunctions

Subordinating conjunctions link dependent clauses, clauses with either a subject or a predicate, to independent clauses, clauses with both a subject and a predicate, to form a complex sentence. The subordinating conjunction will always be at the beginning of the dependent clause. When the dependent clause is at the beginning of the sentence, it will end with a comma. When the independent clause is at the beginning of the sentence, no comma is needed.

Common **subordinating conjunctions** include:

after	since	whenever
although	so that	where
because	unless	wherever
before	until	whether
in order that	when	while

Examples:

> I am hungry *because* I did not eat breakfast.
>
> He went home *when* everyone left.
>
> *While* her brother ate dinner, she played his favorite video game.

Review Video: Subordinating Conjunctions
Visit mometrix.com/academy and enter code: 958913

End Punctuation

Periods

Use a period to end all sentences except direct questions and exclamations. Periods are also used for abbreviations.

> Examples: 3 p.m. | 2 a.m. | Mr. Jones | Mrs. Stevens | Dr. Smith | Bill, Jr. | Pennsylvania Ave.

Note: An abbreviation is a shortened form of a word or phrase.

Question Marks

Question marks should be used following a **direct question**. A polite request can be followed by a period instead of a question mark.

Direct Question: What is for lunch today? | How are you? | Why is that the answer?

Polite Requests: Can you please send me the item tomorrow. | Will you please walk with me on the track.

> **Review Video: Question Marks**
> Visit mometrix.com/academy and enter code: 118471

Exclamation Marks

Exclamation marks are used after a word group or sentence that shows much feeling or has special importance. Exclamation marks should not be overused. They are saved for proper **exclamatory interjections**.

Example: We're going to the finals! | You have a beautiful car! | "That's crazy!" she yelled.

> **Review Video: Exclamation Points**
> Visit mometrix.com/academy and enter code: 199367

Commas

The comma is a punctuation mark that can help you understand connections in a sentence. Not every sentence needs a comma. However, if a sentence needs a comma, you need to put it in the right place. A comma in the wrong place or a missing comma will make a sentence's meaning unclear. These are some of the rules for commas:

Use Case	Example
Before a **coordinating conjunction** joining independent clauses in compound sentences	Bob caught three fish, and I caught two fish.
Between **items in a series**	I will bring the turkey, the pie, and the coffee.
After a **dependent clause** that **begins a complex sentence**	Before she left, Ashley turned off all of the lights in her house.
After **transition words**	Consequently, Joel's mother grounded him.
After an **introductory phrase**	After the final out, we went to a restaurant to celebrate.
After a **prepositional phrase** at the **beginning of a sentence**	At 10 in the evening, Georgia finally arrived home from work.
After an **adverbial clause**	Studying the stars, I was awed by the beauty of the sky.
Before and after **nonessential modifiers**	John Frank, who coaches the team, was promoted today.
Before and after **nonessential appositives**	Thomas Edison, an American inventor, was born in Ohio.
Before and after **nonrestrictive phrases** or **clauses**	His favorite movie, which premiered before he was born, is over three hours long.
After **absolute phrases**	Relieved the test was over, Leah dropped her pencil and slouched in her chair.

COMMAS FOR SETTING OFF NONESSENTIAL WORDS, PHRASES, AND CLAUSES

Identifying where to place commas for nonessential words, phrases, and clauses is sometimes tricky. If the word, phrase, or clause is necessary for the sentence to be complete or logical, then it is essential, or restrictive. Additionally, if the word, phrase, or clause cannot be removed without changing the meaning of the sentence, then it is essential. Nonessential words, phrases, and clauses are those that give unnecessary information or do not flow smoothly with the rest of the words in the sentence. These words usually can also be logically placed in more than one spot in the sentence. **Appositives** are often nonessential words or phrases. They are most often used to specify which person or thing is being discussed. An appositive is an additional name or description that may be essential or nonessential.

> **Review Video: When To Use a Comma**
> Visit mometrix.com/academy and enter code: 786797

EXAMPLE

> The singer growing more exhausted with every song decided to stop dancing and stood still while singing.

Identify the nonrestrictive phrase that should be set off by commas in the above sentence.

a. The singer growing more exhausted
b. Decided to stop dancing
c. Growing more exhausted with every song
d. Stop dancing and stood still

Choice A says that *the singer growing more exhausted* is the nonrestrictive phrase. Is the sentence still a complete sentence without this phrase? No, because choice A includes the subject, *the singer*. Choice A is not the nonrestrictive phrase.

Choice B says that *decided to stop dancing* is the nonrestrictive phrase. Does the sentence make sense without this phrase? No, removing this phrase leaves the following sentence: The singer growing more exhausted with every song and stood still while singing. This is not a logical sentence, so choice B is not the nonrestrictive phrase.

Choice C says that *growing more exhausted with every song* is the nonrestrictive phrase. Removing this phrase leaves the following sentence: The singer decided to stop dancing and stood still while singing. This sentence makes sense and has the same meaning as the original sentence. This phrase gives extra information that is not essential to the sentence, so choice C is the nonrestrictive phrase. Choice C is correct.

Choice D says that *stop dancing and stood still* is the nonrestrictive phrase. Removing this phrase leaves the following sentence: The singer growing more exhausted with every song decided to while singing. This sentence is now missing important information. What did the singer decide to do while singing? The remaining sentence is now missing the verb. Removing choice D makes the sentence incomplete, so choice D is not the nonrestrictive phrase.

EXAMPLE

My friends found a stray cat, which is white and brown and brought it to my house.

Identify the best place for an additional comma in the sentence above?

a. After *friends*
b. After *white*
c. After *brown*
d. After *it*

Choice A says another comma should be added after *friends*. This would set off *found a stray cat*. Can this information be removed from the sentence? No, because the sentence would not make sense without this information. The phrase tells what the friends found. Choice A is incorrect.

Choice B says another comma should be added after *white*. This would set off *which is white*. These words cannot be removed from the sentence because the remaining sentence is not logical. Choice B is incorrect.

Choice C says another comma should be added after *brown*. This would set off the clause *which is white and brown*. Can this information be removed from the sentence? Yes, it can! This information is not necessary for the sentence to make sense, and it does not flow with the rest of the sentence. When this information is removed, the remaining sentence is logical and complete, and it flows well. Choice C is correct.

Choice D says another comma should be added after *it*. This would set off *which is white and brown and brought it*. These words cannot be removed from the sentence because the remaining words do not form a logical sentence. Choice D is incorrect.

SEMICOLONS

The semicolon is used to connect major sentence pieces of equal value. Some rules for semicolons include:

Use Case	Example
Between closely connected independent clauses **not connected with a coordinating conjunction**	You are right; we should go with your plan.
Between independent clauses **linked with a transitional word**	I think that we can agree on this; however, I am not sure about my friends.
Between items in a **series that has internal punctuation**	I have visited New York, New York; Augusta, Maine; and Baltimore, Maryland.

Review Video: How to Use Semicolons
Visit mometrix.com/academy and enter code: 370605

EXAMPLE

Which of the following sentences is NOT written correctly?

a. My sister burned the lasagna we were going to eat for dinner; we went out to eat instead of cooking something else.
b. The ball rolled into the ditch, therefore, it was muddy and wet when he retrieved it.
c. She has lived in many cities, including Nashville, Tennessee; San Diego, California; and Salt Lake City, Utah.
d. He hung the picture in the wrong spot; now there is a distracting hole in the wall.

Choice A is a compound sentence. The semicolon is used to separate two independent clauses. There is no coordinating conjunction in the sentence. This sentence correctly uses a semicolon, so choice A is incorrect.

Choice B is a compound sentence. In a compound sentence, either a coordinating conjunction or a semicolon can be used to separate the independent clauses. This sentence includes a transitional word, but it uses neither a semicolon nor a coordinating conjunction. To revise this sentence, *therefore* can be replaced by a coordinating conjunction, or the first comma can be replaced with a semicolon This sentence is written incorrectly, so choice B is the correct answer.

Choice C is a sentence that includes a list. Remember that semicolons can be used to separate items in a list when at least one of the items includes a comma. In this sentence, a list of cities is given. Since a comma is required to separate the name of a city from the name of the state it is in, each of the items in the list contain a comma. This means that each full city name must be separated by a semicolon. This sentence is written correctly, so choice C is incorrect.

Choice D is a compound sentence and does not contain a coordinating conjunction. Semicolons can be used to separate independent clauses in a compound sentence instead of a coordinating conjunction. This sentence uses a semicolon correctly, so choice D is incorrect.

Colons

The colon is used to call attention to the words that follow it. A colon must come after a **complete independent clause**. The rules for colons are as follows:

Use Case	Example
After an independent clause to **make a list**	I want to learn many languages: Spanish, German, and Italian.
For **explanations**	There is one thing that stands out on your resume: responsibility.
To give a **quote**	He started with an idea: "We are able to do more than we imagine."
After the **greeting in a formal letter**	To Whom It May Concern:
Show **hours and minutes**	It is 3:14 p.m.
Separate a **title and subtitle**	The essay is titled "America: A Short Introduction to a Modern Country."

Review Video: Using Colons
Visit mometrix.com/academy and enter code: 868673

Example

Which of the following sentences does NOT use a colon correctly?

a. Your reports must be submitted by 10:30 p.m.
b. Terrence: his best friend, is graduating from college on Saturday.
c. Shelly had three tasks to complete before her mother returned: empty the dishwasher, walk the dog, and tidy the living room.
d. Brian was excited to write a report over his favorite book: *Frankenstein*.

Choice A uses a colon to separate the hour from the minute. Colons are necessary when writing hours and minutes. This colon is used correctly and is in the right place, so choice A is incorrect.

Choice B uses a colon to separate a nonessential appositive. This is not an acceptable use for a colon because it is not used in a time, and it does not follow an independent clause. Also, nonessential appositives that appear in the middle of a sentence should only be set off by commas. This is an incorrect use for a colon, so choice B is the correct answer.

Choice C uses a colon to separate an independent clause from a list. This is an acceptable use for a colon. This colon is appropriately used and is in the right place, so choice C is incorrect.

Choice D uses a colon for explanation. This is an acceptable use for a colon when the word, phrase, or clause being separated follows an independent clause. The independent clause should also introduce, or describe, the information following the colon. Choice D correctly uses a colon, so it is incorrect.

PARENTHESES

Parentheses are used for additional information. Also, they can be used to put labels for letters or numbers in a series. Parentheses should not be used very often. If they are overused, parentheses can be a distraction instead of a help.

Examples:

> **Extra Information**: The rattlesnake (see Image 2) is a dangerous snake of North and South America.
>
> **Series**: Include in the email (1) your name, (2) your address, and (3) your question for the author.

Review Video: Parentheses
Visit mometrix.com/academy and enter code: 947743

EXAMPLE

Which of the following CANNOT be set off by parentheses?

a. A short list of examples
b. A reference to a graph or chart that is relevant to the text
c. An essential phrase in a sentence
d. A number used to label an item in a series

Remember that parentheses are used to set off extra information from the rest of the sentence. Extra words set off by parentheses are often not meant to be read with the rest of the sentence in the same way as words set off by commas. Usually, the words in parenthesis do not impact the meaning of the other words in the sentence. Instead, they can include additional information that is relevant to the sentence or guide the reader to that information.

Choice A says that parentheses cannot be used to set off a short list of examples. Examples are used to elaborate on information and help the reader better understand it. Examples often do not impact the meaning of the sentence. When there are only a few examples and they do not affect the sentence's meaning, they can be set off by parentheses.

Choice B says that parentheses cannot be used to set off a reference to a graph or chart. References like these are used to lead the reader to look at a graph or chart so he or she will see important information. This keeps the writer from placing the image in between sections of text. When references are in parentheses, they are not meant to impact the meaning of the sentence. References to graphs and charts can be set off by parentheses.

Choice C says that parentheses cannot be used to set off essential phrases in a sentence. When a phrase is essential to a sentence, it should not be set off by any punctuation marks. Essential phrases cannot be set off by parentheses, so choice C is correct.

Choice D says that parentheses cannot be used to set off numbers used as labels. Sometimes, when a list appears in a sentence, the items may be referred to in a different location. In these cases, it can be helpful when the items are labeled. The labels are meant to guide the readers to the information, not to change the meaning of the sentence. Numbers used to label items in a series can be set off by parentheses.

Quotation Marks

Use quotation marks to close off **direct quotations** of a person's written or spoken words, which are also called **dialogue**. Do not use quotation marks around indirect quotations. An indirect quotation gives someone's message without using the person's exact words. Use **single quotation marks** to close off a quotation inside a quotation.

> **Direct Quote**: Nancy said, "I am waiting for Henry to arrive."
>
> **Indirect Quote**: Henry said that he is going to be late to the meeting.
>
> **Quote inside a Quote**: The teacher asked, "Has everyone read Martin Luther King's 'I Have a Dream' speech?"

Quotation marks should be used around the titles of **short works**: newspaper and magazine articles, poems, short stories, songs, television episodes, and radio programs. Titles of **long works** should be italicized when they are part of a typed composition or underlined when they are part of a handwritten composition.

Examples:

> "Rip Van Winkle" (short story by Washington Irving)
>
> "O Captain! My Captain!" (poem by Walt Whitman)

Review Video: Quotation Marks
Visit mometrix.com/academy and enter code: 884918

Apostrophes

An apostrophe is used to show **possession** or the **deletion of letters in contractions**. An apostrophe is not needed with the possessive pronouns *his, hers, its, ours, theirs, whose*, and *yours*.

Singular Nouns: David's car | a book's theme | my brother's board game

Plural Nouns that end with *-s*: the scissors' handle | boys' basketball

Plural Nouns that end without *-s*: Men's department | the people's adventure

Review Video: Apostrophes
Visit mometrix.com/academy and enter code: 213068

Review Video: Punctuation Errors in Possessive Pronouns
Visit mometrix.com/academy and enter code: 221438

Apostrophes in Contractions

Contractions are combinations of words. Contractions involve taking two words, removing at least one letter from one of the words, putting an apostrophe in its place, and removing the space. For example, *does not* can be written as the contraction *doesn't*. The *o* is removed from *not* and is replaced with an apostrophe, which represents the removed letter, so it appears as *n't*. The space after does is then removed, turning *does not* into the contraction *doesn't*. Some more examples of contractions are listed below.

First Word	Second Word	Contraction
Can	Not	Can't
Do	Not	Don't
She	Will	She'll
They	Will	They'll
He	Is	He's
It	Is	It's
They	Are	They're
I	Am	I'm

Not all words can be used to form contractions, but many small, commonly used words can.

Capitalization

One important part of using correct grammar is properly capitalizing words. Usually, only nouns will be capitalized, but there are some exceptions. The most important capitalization rule is that the first word of every sentence, no matter what part of speech it is, should be capitalized. Another exception is that the pronoun *I* should always be capitalized.

Proper nouns are always capitalized, but sometimes it can be tricky to decide whether or not a noun is a proper noun. Some words that are usually common nouns may become proper nouns when used with other words or phrases. Also, when words that are not nouns are used with a noun, or when a group of words are used together as one noun, those words may also need to be capitalized.

Titles of Books, Stories, and Essays

Most of the words in titles of things like books, stories, and essays should be capitalized, but some should not. The very first word in a title should always be capitalized. Any other word in a title that is a noun, pronoun, adjective, verb or adverb should be capitalized. Articles, such as *a* or *the*, should not be capitalized. Short conjunctions and prepositions are usually not capitalized.

Abbreviations, Initials, and Acronyms

Abbreviations are shortened versions of other words. When an abbreviation shortens, or abbreviates, a word that should be capitalized, the abbreviation's first letter should also be capitalized. When the shortened word is a noun that is not capitalized, the abbreviation should be in lowercase. Initials are usually written using the first letter from multiple words. For example, John Fitzgerald Kennedy is commonly referred to by his initials, JFK. Acronyms also use the first letter from multiple words, but they are different from initials because they form words on their own. For example, NASA is an acronym for National Aeronautics and Space Administration. Some acronyms, like NASA, omit small words, such as *and*, *of*, and *for*. When initials and acronyms are used for proper nouns, each letter should be capitalized.

The types of words and phrases in the chart below are proper nouns and should always be capitalized:

	Description	**Example**
Historical Periods	A range of time in history that is related to specific events or circumstances	During the Romantic Period, many authors and poets wrote about their emotions.
Historical Events	Names of important events that happened in history	Napoleon Bonaparte led France after the French Revolution.
Historical Documents	Titles of important papers or compositions that are connected to historical events	The Mayflower Compact was written to create rules and expectations for the colony in Plymouth.
Languages	Names of the different languages that people speak	I want to learn to speak Cantonese, Spanish, and German.
Races and Ethnicities	Words often used to describe a person's heritage or cultural group	Malia taught her granddaughter how to hula so she could share a tradition of her Native Hawaiian heritage with her.
Nationalities	Words that describe which country a person is from	My teacher who moved to Canada last year is Romanian.
Organizations	Titles of official groups formed by people	Fewer than half of the states in America have a team in the National Basketball Association.

Example

> Allison and Claire enjoy studying art from the beginning of the renaissance. They started a club so they and other students can learn more about it. Allison and Claire named the club Early Renaissance Art Club, which can be abbreviated to ERA Club. The students that joined elected Claire as the president and Allison as the vice president. The club's first meeting will take place after Christmas vacation.

Which of the following changes should be made in the passage?

a. In the first sentence, *Renaissance* should be capitalized.
b. In the third sentence, *ERA* should be written as *Era*.
c. In the fourth sentence, *president* and *vice president* should be capitalized.
d. In the last sentence, *Christmas* should be in lowercase.

Choice A says that *Renaissance* should be capitalized in the first sentence of the passage. The Renaissance is a historical period, so *Renaissance* is a proper noun that should always be capitalized. Choice A is correct.

Choice B says that *ERA* should be written as *Era*. In the third sentence of the passage, the word *era* is used as an acronym. Remember that all letters in an acronym should be capitalized. The correct capitalization is *ERA*, so choice B is incorrect.

Choice C says that *president* and *vice president* should be capitalized. Titles for people are capitalized when they are used as part of a person's name or in the place of a person's name. In this passage, these titles are not used as part of anyone's name or in place of anyone's name, so they should be in lowercase. Choice C is incorrect.

Choice D says that *Christmas* should be in lowercase. The passage says that the first meeting will be held after Christmas break. Even though *Christmas* is used to describe when the students are getting a vacation from school, it is the name of a holiday. Names of holidays are always capitalized, so choice D is incorrect.

Word Confusion

To, Too, and Two

To can be an adverb or a preposition for showing direction, purpose, and relationship. A dictionary can also be used to see the many other ways to use *to* in a sentence.

> Examples: I went to the store. | I want to go with you.

Too is an adverb that means *also, as well, very,* or *in excess.*

> Examples: I can walk a mile too. | You have eaten too much.

Two is a number.

> Example: You have two minutes left.

There, Their, and They're

There can be an adjective, adverb, or pronoun. Often, *there* is used to show a place or to start a sentence.

> Examples: I went there yesterday. | There is something in his pocket.

Their is a pronoun that is used to show ownership.

Examples: He is their father. | This is their fourth apology this week.

They're is a contraction of *they are.*

Example: Did you know that they're in town?

Its and It's

Its is a possessive pronoun that shows ownership.

Example: The guitar is in its case.

It's is a contraction of *it is.*

Example: It's an honor and a privilege to meet you.

Affect and Effect

There are two main reasons that *affect* and *effect* are so often confused: 1) both words can be used as either a noun or a verb, and 2) unlike most homophones, their usage and meanings are closely related to each other. Here is a quick explanation of the four usage options:

Affect (n): feeling, emotion, or mood that is displayed

Example: The patient had a flat *affect.* (i.e., his face showed little or no emotion)

Affect (v): to alter, to change, to influence

Example: The sunshine *affects* the plant's growth.

Effect (n): a result, a consequence

Example: What *effect* will this weather have on our schedule?

Effect (v): to bring about, to cause to be

Example: These new rules will *effect* order in the office.

Example

Choose the correct spelling from each pair of homophones in the following passage.

I found a unique tree in the forest. (It's/Its) trunk is blue, and it has (two/too) many branches to count. I brought some of my friends to see it, but the tree did not seem to (affect/effect) them. While (their/they're) not fascinated by the strange tree, I am!

The first pair of homophones is *it's* and *its*. Remember that the contraction *it's* is used in place of *it is. Its* is a possessive pronoun that shows a thing's ownership or possession. An easy way to decide whether *it's* or *its* is correct is to see how the sentence sounds with *it is*, instead. *It is trunk is blue* does not make sense. *Its trunk is blue* means that the tree has a blue trunk, so *its* is the correct choice.

The next pair of homophones is *two* and *too*. *Two* only means the number two. *Too* can mean *also* or *in excess*. Which of these makes the most sense in this sentence? *Two many branches to count* or *too many branches to count*? The correct meaning is that there is an abundance of branches, so *too* is the correct choice for this pair.

The third pair of homophones is *affect* and *effect*. Since both of these words can be used as a noun or verb, identifying the correct part of speech is a helpful first step. The part of speech is a verb, since the correct word will show what *the tree* does to *them*. *Affect* as a verb means to change or influence. *Effect* as a verb means to lead to or cause something to happen. Replace the homophone with these synonyms. Seeing the tree cannot cause or lead the speaker's friends to exist, but it can change them or influence them. *Affect* is the correct choice for this pair.

The last pair of homophones is *their* and *they're*. *Their* is a possessive pronoun used to show that multiple people or things own something. *They're* is a contraction used in place of *they are*. Replace the homophone with *they are*. Does the sentence make sense? It does because they, the speaker's friends, are not fascinated by the tree. Saying *their not fascinated* does not make sense. *They're* is the correct choice for this pair.

Types of Essays

Essays

Essays usually focus on one topic, subject, or goal. There are several types of essays, including informative, persuasive, and narrative. An essay's structure and formality depend on the type of essay and its goal. While narrative essays typically do not include outside sources, other types of essays often require some research and the use of primary and secondary sources.

The basic format of an essay typically has three major parts: the introduction, the body, and the conclusion. The body is further divided into the writer's main points. Most essays will have at least three main points, but essays that go into more depth can have almost any number of main points.

An essay's introduction should answer three questions:

1. What is the **subject** of the essay?

   If an essay is about a book, the answer would include the title and author of the book, as well as any additional information needed, such as the subject or argument of the book.

2. How does the essay **discuss** the subject?

   To answer this, the writer briefly summarizes the main points and the evidence supporting them to let readers know how the essay is organized and what information they can expect to read.

3. What will the essay **prove**?

   This information is in the thesis statement, usually the opening paragraph's last sentence, which clearly states the writer's message.

The body elaborates on all the main points related to the thesis, introducing one main point at a time, and includes supporting evidence with each main point. Each body paragraph should state the point in a topic sentence, which is usually the first sentence in the paragraph. The paragraph should then explain the point's meaning, support it with quotations or other evidence, and then explain how this point and the evidence are related to the thesis. The writer should then repeat this procedure in a new paragraph for each additional main point.

The conclusion restates the content of the introduction, including the thesis, to remind the reader of the essay's main argument or subject. The essay writer may also summarize the highlights of the argument or description contained in the body of the essay, following the same organization originally used in the body. For example, a conclusion might look like: Point 1 + Point 2 + Point 3 = Thesis, or Point 1 → Point 2 → Point 3 → Thesis Proof. Good organization makes essays easier for writers to compose and provides a guide for readers to follow. Well-organized essays hold attention better and are more likely to get readers to believe or agree with the writer.

Using Sources in Essays

Sometimes writers use information from others in their work. This is most common in expository and persuasive writing. For an expository essay, a writer may not know all of the information that he or she needs to finish the composition. The writer may use other people's work to find the missing information and complete the composition. Persuasive writers may do research to find facts or statements from others that support their own beliefs and make their writing more persuasive. In both cases, research helps the writer find information that **supports** his or her **original work**.

Outside information must be relevant, true, and helpful to be appropriate for a composition. Writers must also be careful not to use too much outside information, since this can make the composition unoriginal. If a writer does use outside information, it is extremely important that the writer mention in the composition where the information came from. If the writer forgets or chooses not to say where the information came from, he or she has stolen someone else's work and presented it as their own. Doing this is called **plagiarism**.

Informational Texts

Informational texts, also called instructional or expository texts, are compositions written to inform the reader about a specific topic. An informational essay can inform readers in a variety of ways, such as giving them instructions, telling them facts about the topic, or teaching them why something happens. Informational texts should be logical, meaning that they should present information in an order that the reader can easily understand, and they should include the right amount of information so the writer successfully informs his or her audience of new information.

Informational texts should also focus on a **central idea**. In the introduction of an informational text, there may be a sentence or two that clearly state the essay's central idea. This sentence, or sentences, is called a **thesis statement**. The central idea should be clear throughout the composition. By emphasizing the central idea in the introduction, body, and conclusion, the writer can ensure that the central idea is clear. One way to make sure that the central idea is emphasized is to think about the purpose of each part of the essay. The introduction prepares the reader by telling them what the rest of the essay is about, so the central idea should be **introduced** in this section. The body tells the reader the information the writer wants to tell the audience, so this **explains** the central idea and facts about it to the reader. The conclusion is used to **remind** the reader of how the information in the body is related and **restates** the central idea one final time.

Structures or Organizational Patterns in Informational Texts

Informational text can be **descriptive**, meaning that it gives information that can be experienced through the five senses, or it answers the questions what, who, when, where, and why. One common method of organizing informational text is to put it in a certain sequence, or order. **Chronological** texts include events in the order that they occurred, from start to finish. **How-to**, or **instructional**, texts organize information into a series of instructions in the order in which the steps should be followed. **Comparison-contrast** structures of informational text describe different ideas to their readers by pointing out how things or ideas are similar and how they are different. **Cause and effect** structures of informational text describe events that occurred and the causes or reasons for those events. **Problem and solution** structures of informational texts introduce and describe problems and offer one or more solutions for each problem described.

ARGUMENTATIVE WRITING

In argumentative writing, the writer expresses a belief or opinion that he or she wants to lead readers to agree with. When writing an argumentative composition, the writer should first identify the **topic** his or her opinion is about. The topic may be serious or fun, as long as there is one clear topic in the composition. The next step is for the writer to determine his or her opinion on the topic and determine why he or she holds that opinion. In order to persuade others to agree with their opinion, the writer must be able to give readers reasons to support the opinion. If the writer does not know why he or she has an opinion, it will be difficult to convince readers to agree. In addition to having reasons that support their opinion, writers should prepare examples that support each of these reasons in order to strengthen their composition.

Once the writer has determined his or her topic, opinion, and reasons for having the opinion, he or she is ready to begin writing an argumentative essay. In the introduction, the writer should capture the reader's interest, introduce the topic, and reveal his or her opinion about the topic. In the body of the composition, the writer should remind the reader of the opinion and give his or her reasons for holding the opinion. If the writer has any examples, facts, or other information that supports his or her opinion or reasons for believing it, these should also be included in the body. Writers may also use a body paragraph to mention opposing opinions or beliefs and explain why they disagree with them. As in other compositions, the conclusion should remind the reader of the essay's topic and purpose, as well as remind the reader how the opinion has been explained and supported. The conclusion should also invite the reader to continue thinking about the topic and writer's opinion. This can be done through questions or statements that lead readers to consider whether or not they agree with the author's opinion or what their own opinions are.

Review Video: Argumentative Writing
Visit mometrix.com/academy and enter code: 561544

INFORMATIVE VS. PERSUASIVE WRITING

Informative writing, also called explanatory or expository writing, is written to show that something is true or factual, while **persuasive** writing is written to lead the reader to agree with something that may or may not be true or factual. While persuasive text is written to **persuade** readers to agree with the author's position, informative text simply **provides information** to readers. Informative writing **informs** readers about why or how something is as it is. This can include offering new information, explaining how a process works, or describing a concept for readers.

Review Video: Informational Text
Visit mometrix.com/academy and enter code: 924964

FACTS AND OPINIONS

Writers and readers must always be aware of the difference between fact and opinion. A **fact** can be tested and proven to be true. An **opinion**, on the other hand, is someone's personal thoughts or feelings. Opinions are often not changed by information. If an author writes that a newborn elephant is about five times taller than a newborn giraffe, then he or she is stating a fact. If the author writes that giraffes are more interesting than elephants, then he or she is giving an opinion because this cannot be proven to be true or false. Opinions are often supported by facts. For instance, the author might use a comparison between the way that giraffes eat and the way elephants eat as evidence of how giraffes are more interesting. An opinion supported by facts tends to be more convincing. On the other hand, when authors support their opinions with other opinions, readers should seriously think about and read the argument carefully to see whether it is logical and trustworthy.

Review Video: Distinguishing Fact and Opinion
Visit mometrix.com/academy and enter code: 870899

NARRATIVE WRITING

Put simply, **narrative** writing tells a story. Narratives should tell stories in such a way that the readers learn something or gain understanding about a related topic or idea. Personal narratives are narratives writers create about personal experiences that were meaningful to them. Narratives should start with the story's actions or events, rather than long descriptions or introductions. However, the narrative should still include descriptions at points where they will entertain the reader or help the reader visualize or better understand the scene. To write an effective description, writers should include sensory details, asking themselves what they saw, heard, felt or touched, smelled, and tasted during the experiences they describe. In narrative writing, the details should be **concrete** rather than **abstract**. Concrete details are those that can be experienced through one of the five senses, while abstract details are not able to be experienced in this way. Using concrete details enables readers to imagine everything that the writer describes. Writers should make sure that there is a point to each story by describing what they learned from the experience they narrate.

PERSONAL NARRATIVES

A **personal narrative** is a story about something that happened to the writer. **Personal narrative essays** are structured the same as other types of essays, as they have an introduction, body paragraphs, and a conclusion. Like other essays, the introduction of a personal narrative should contain a hook, or an opening sentence that interests the reader and prompts them to read the rest of the narrative. The introduction may also provide context for the story told in the personal narrative. One significant difference between personal narratives and other essays is that the body paragraphs of a personal narrative should contain sensory details, or imagery. A good personal narrative will give the reader a clear picture of the events and engage their emotions, and sensory details are effective at achieving these goals. The body should describe the events in chronological order, and the story should be completed in the last body paragraph. The conclusion will summarize the main idea of the personal narrative and may include information such as the writer's brief reflection on the events, how the events taught or changed the writer, or any relevant events that have happened since the events in the narrative.

SENSORY DETAILS

Writers need to use vivid descriptions when writing descriptive essays. Narratives should also include descriptions of characters, things, and events. Writers should remember to describe not only the visual detail of what someone or something looks like, but details from other senses, as well. For example, they can contrast the feeling of a sea breeze to the feeling of a mountain breeze, describe how they think something inedible would taste, and compare sounds they hear in the same location at different times of day and night. Readers have trouble visualizing images or imagining sensory impressions and feelings from abstract descriptions, so concrete descriptions make these more real.

Informational Text Example

Below is a prompt for an informational text. There is also an example of an essay that addresses the prompt. There are multiple drafts of this essay to show what kinds of changes a writer may make during the writing process to improve his or her work.

PROMPT:

Do you ever dream of going to a new city, state, or even country? Write about one place you want to travel to on vacation. Be sure to share why you would like to visit that place.

Rough Draft

Imagine traveling into the city or the beach and being transported back in time. This is what it must be like to live in Greece. The old buildings, beautiful beaches, and Greek foods are reasons I want to visit Greece.

Several buildings from ancient Greece are still standing, and they can easily be enjoyed by visitors and the people of Greece today. Some of the most famous ones, like the Parthenon, are located throughout the capital. This means that even when you are sitting in an air-conditioned restaurant in Athens, you can still see what is left of history. There are also tours that teach visitors more about these structures and the events that happened at each one. Though seeing these structures is not the only reason I would like to visit Greece, they would be enough of a reason for me to visit.

In addition to the scenery, another reason to visit Greece is to try real Greek and Mediterranean foods. I have tried a few Greek foods, like baklava and pita bread, and I enjoyed them. While these foods are available in America, I think they are probably made a little differently in Greece. I am interested in seeing what the differences are and trying new things. I hope I can visit Greece soon, because I am getting hungry just thinking about the food there!

Greece has a variety of beaches, as some are small with rocky structures and some look like normal beaches. The water is also different from some American waters because Greece is next to the Mediterranean Sea. Also, many historical events and myths took place on some of the beaches. I would love to sit on one of those beaches and try to imagine ships or characters from myths coming to the shore! The beaches in Greece are beautiful, but I think they also sound fun and interesting!

Walking through historical structures, visiting unique beaches, and eating new foods there is my dream. If I only ever have the chance to go on one vacation, I hope it is to Greece!

Revised Draft

Imagine traveling into the city or the beach and being transported back in time. This is what it must be like to live in Greece. <u>The remaining historical sites that are still there allow visitors to see two cultures side by side.</u> The old buildings, beautiful beaches, and Greek foods are reasons I want to visit Greece.

Several buildings from ancient Greece are still standing, and they can easily be enjoyed by visitors and the people of Greece today. Some of the most famous ones, like the Parthenon, are located throughout the capital. This means that even when you are sitting in an air-conditioned restaurant in Athens, you can still see what is left of history. There are also tours that teach visitors more about these structures and the events that happened at each one. Though seeing these structures is not the only reason I would like to visit Greece, they would be enough of a reason for me to visit.

Greece has a variety of beaches, as some are small with rocky structures and some look like normal beaches. The water is also different from some American waters because Greece is next to the Mediterranean Sea. Also, many historical events and myths took place on some of the beaches. I would love to sit on one of those beaches and try to imagine ships or characters from myths coming to the shore! The beaches in Greece are beautiful, but I think they also sound fun and interesting!

In addition to the scenery, a third reason to visit Greece is to try real Greek and Mediterranean foods. I have tried a few Greek foods, like baklava and pita bread, and I enjoyed them. While these foods are available in America, I think they are probably made a little differently in Greece. I am interested in seeing what the differences are and trying new things. I hope I can visit Greece soon, because I am getting hungry just thinking about the food there!

<u>Greece is a special place where the old and the new come together.</u> Walking through historical structures, visiting unique beaches, and eating new foods there is my dream. If I only ever have the chance to go on one vacation, I hope it is to Greece!

Revised Draft Notes

Remember the purpose of the revising stage of the writing process. When revising, it is important to look at the whole composition. Do all of the paragraphs strengthen the composition? Do the introduction and conclusion help the reader understand the central idea and main points?

In this revision, nothing has been removed, but there are some additions. Look at the underlined words. In the introduction, a sentence has been added. Why? Previously, the introduction had only a hook and a thesis. The sentences were well written, but the writer did not provide a connection between the hook and the thesis. The new sentence connects the ideas in both sentences and introduces some of the main points the writer will discuss in the essay.

In the conclusion, another sentence has been added. This sentence strengthens the composition by creating a transition from the body to the conclusion. Before, the conclusion began abruptly by listing the three main points from the body of the essay. This sentence makes the essay flow better by giving the reader a transition from the body to the conclusion. This sentence reminds the reader of composition's central idea before repeating the writer's main points and sharing his or her hopes.

Finally, the third and fourth paragraphs have been switched. Why is that? Before, the writer discussed ancient buildings, then food, then the beaches. This revised draft discusses buildings, then beaches, then food. This new order puts the more closely related points, the scenery of the buildings and beaches, closer together in the essay. This helps the reader by making the organization of the essay more logical.

Edited Draft

Imagine traveling into the city or the beach and being transported back in time. This is what it must be like to live in <u>Greece, since the remaining</u> historical sites ~~that are still there~~ allow visitors to see two cultures side by side. The ~~old~~ <u>ancient</u> buildings, beautiful beaches, and Greek foods are reasons I want to visit Greece.

Several buildings from ancient Greece are still standing, and they can easily be enjoyed by visitors and the people of Greece today. Some of the most famous ones, like the Parthenon, are located throughout the capital. This means that even when you are sitting in an air-conditioned restaurant in Athens, you can still see ~~what is left~~ <u>glimpses</u> of history. There are also tours that teach visitors more about these structures and the events that happened at each one. ~~Though seeing these structures is not the only reason I would like to visit Greece, they would be enough of a reason for me to visit.~~ <u>Seeing these structures alone is enough of a reason for me to visit Greece!</u>

<u>Another reason I want to travel to Greece is to see the beaches there. There are</u> a variety of beaches, as some are small with rocky structures and some look like ~~normal~~ <u>typical</u> beaches. The water is also different from some American waters because Greece is next to the Mediterranean Sea. Also, many historical events and myths took place on some of the beaches. I would love to sit on one of those beaches and try to imagine ships or characters from myths coming to the shore! The beaches in Greece are beautiful, but I think they also sound fun and interesting!

In addition to the scenery, a third reason to visit Greece is to try ~~real~~ <u>authentic</u> Greek and Mediterranean foods. I have tried a few Greek foods, like baklava and pita bread, and I enjoyed them. While these foods are available in America, I think they are probably made a little differently in Greece<u>, so</u> I am interested in seeing what the differences are and trying new things. I hope I can visit Greece soon, because I am getting hungry just thinking about the food there!

Greece is a special place where the old and the new come together. Walking through historical structures, visiting unique beaches, and eating new foods there is my dream. If I only ever have the chance to go on one vacation, I hope it is to Greece!

Edited Draft Notes

Since the writer has revised his or her work, the next step is to edit the composition. Remember that editing is very similar to revising, but editing usually includes paying attention to each paragraph, instead of the whole composition. Look at the changes that were made to each paragraph.

There are small changes throughout this draft. First, look at the introduction. Before, the introduction had four sentences that were about the same length. In this draft, the second and third sentences have been combined to make a longer sentence. This creates more sentence variety in the introduction, which makes the composition more entertaining for the writer's audience. A few words have been crossed out, as well. *That are still there* has been replaced with *remaining*. This change makes the writing more concise and formal. Also, *old* has been replaced with *ancient*. This clarifies what kind of buildings the writer is describing by using a word that more specifically describes the age of the buildings.

In the next paragraph, *what is left* has been replaced with *glimpses*. This change makes the writing more concise by using one word instead of three. Furthermore, this change makes the writing more interesting and entertaining by using a better vocabulary word. At the end of the paragraph, the last sentence has been condensed. Most of the sentences in this paragraph are long. Shortening this sentence adds sentence variety to this paragraph and makes the concluding sentence more concise. Overall, these changes make the paragraph easier to read by eliminating unnecessary words and using better vocabulary.

There are a few more changes left in the third and fourth paragraphs. A transition has been added to the beginning of the third paragraph. Now, the writer introduces the next main point before describing the beaches. This makes the essay flow better overall and making it easier for the writer's audience to read. *Normal* has been replaced with *typical*. Since there are so many different beaches in the world, there are not really any normal beaches. *Typical* is a much clearer word. Now, the reader knows that the writer is trying to distinguish the beaches in Greece from the type of beaches that he or she sees most often.

In the next paragraph, *real* has been replaced with *authentic*. The food the writer has tried in America has been real food, not fake food, so this is poor word choice. Now, *authentic* clarifies the writer's meaning that the food will be closer to its original Greek or Mediterranean style. These changes in word choice improve the clarity of the essay by using specific words that better communicate the writer's points. Finally, the third and fourth sentences have been joined together. This increases sentence variety by adding a longer sentence to this paragraph.

FINAL DRAFT

Imagine traveling into the city or the beach and being transported back in time. This is what it must be like to live in Greece, since the remaining historical sites allow visitors to see two cultures side by side. The ancient buildings, beautiful beaches, and Greek foods are reasons I want to visit Greece.

Several buildings from ancient Greece are still standing, and they can easily be enjoyed by visitors and the people of Greece today. Some of the most famous ones, like the Parthenon, are located throughout the capital. This means that even when you are sitting in an air-conditioned restaurant in Athens, you can still see glimpses of history. There are also tours that teach visitors more about these structures and the events that happened at each one. Seeing these structures alone is enough of a reason for me to visit Greece!

Another reason I want to travel to Greece is to see the beaches there. There are a variety of beaches, as some are small with rocky structures and some look like typical beaches. The water is also different from some American waters because Greece is next to the Mediterranean Sea. Also, many historical events and myths took place on some of the beaches. I would love to sit on one of those beaches and try to imagine ships or characters from myths coming to the shore! The beaches in Greece are beautiful, but I think they also sound fun and interesting!

In addition to the scenery, a third reason to visit Greece is to try authentic Greek and Mediterranean foods. I have tried a few Greek foods, like baklava and pita bread, and I enjoyed them. While these foods are available in America, I think they are probably made a little differently in Greece, so I am interested in seeing what the differences are and trying new things. I hope I can visit Greece soon, because I am getting hungry just thinking about the food there!

Greece is a special place where the old and the new come together. Walking through historical structures, visiting unique beaches, and eating new foods there is my dream. If I only ever have the chance to go on one vacation, I hope it is to Greece!

Final Draft Evaluation

The essay answers the prompt and is on topic throughout the composition. The central idea is clear and is stated in the introduction, supported in the body, and restated in the conclusion. The thesis statement restates parts of the prompt and gives the reader a preview of the rest of the essay. The body uses well-structured paragraphs to explain the supporting details and examples and connects them to the central idea. The conclusion also emphasizes the central idea and supporting details and invites the reader to consider what they have read.

The essay is also interesting and written with a variety of sentence types. It uses transitions and good paragraph structure to make the essay easy for the reader to understand. The introduction also uses a hook to get the reader's attention and help him or her relate to the information in the essay. Not only does this essay answer the prompt and have appropriate structure, but it also makes use of good, engaging, and interesting details.

Practice Test #1

Questions 1-8 pertain to the following passage:

An American Hero

(1) In the year 1912, the unsinkable Titanic sank, the United States territory of Arizona became a state, and my Great Uncle Charlie was born. (2) Charlie was born in a small town in Kentucky. (3) On a farm. (4) He grew up learning about the seasons, when to plant the seeds, and when the crops were ripe for picking. (5) His mornings were spent with his hands in dirt as he tended to the growing corps.

(6) When Charlie was only 12, his father died. (7) He had to quit school to take care of his family. (8) While other children were learning and playing at school, Charlie worked in factories to help pay for his mother and sisters to eat. (9) Irregardless of how he felt about having to work, Charlie never complained.

(10) On December 7, 1941, Japan attacked the American naval base at Pearl Harbor. (11) Charlie enlisted in the army when he was 30 years old, and went to fight in the war. (12) He fought in six major battles, including landing in Normandy on D-Day. (13) While he was in the army, Charlie joined the United States horseshoe team and became the champion of the european allies. (14) After the war, Charlie returned to Kentucky married a woman named Bethany, and had three children.

(15) Today, Charlie can still be found with his hands in the dirt. (16) He loves to work in the small garden beside his front porch. (17) The bright colors of ripening strawberries, tomatoes, and ears of corn can be seen next to the house with Charlie walking though the rows of crops with his watering can. (18) He tends to them with love. (19) Charlie watches over his family like the crops in the garden, and that is why he is my hero.

1. What is the BEST way to explain the information in sentences 2 and 3?

a. Charlie was born in a small town in Kentucky. It was on a farm
b. Charlie was born in Kentucky. In a small town and on a farm
c. Charlie was born in a small town. In Kentucky, it was on a farm
d. Charlie was born in a small Kentucky town on a farm

2. What change, if any, should be made to sentence 5?

a. Change *corps* to *crops*
b. Change *were* to *was*
c. Insert a comma after *dirt*
d. Make no change

3. What change, if any, should be made to sentence 9?

a. Change *complained* to *complains*
b. Change *irregardless* to *regardless*
c. Delete the comma after *work*
d. Make no change

4. What sentence could BEST follow and support sentence 10?

a. Pearl Harbor is a naval base in Hawaii
b. The USS Arizona was one of the battleships that sank
c. This event directly led into the United States' involvement in World War II
d. Charlie had never been to Hawaii

5. What change, if any, should be made to sentence 13?

a. Change *european* to *European*
b. Change *became* to *becomes*
c. Insert a comma after *champion*
d. Make no change

6. What change, if any, should be made to sentence 14?

a. Change *returned* to *returns*
b. Insert a comma after *Kentucky*
c. Insert *and* after *Kentucky*
d. Make no change

7. What change, if any, should be made in sentence 16?

a. Change *loves* to *loved*
b. Insert a comma after *garden*
c. Change *beside* to *besides*
d. Make no change

8. What change, if any, should be made in sentence 17?

a. Change *colors* to *colours*
b. Delete the comma after *strawberries*
c. Change *though* to *through*
d. Make no change

Questions 9 – 16 pertain to the following story:

The Top Deck

(1) We walked outside through the sliding glass doors and waited in line for the large, double-decker red bus. (2) My family flew to London for a week in July to celebrate my sisters graduation. (3) She wore a blue cap and gown. (4) The sky was gray, and light puddles spotted the ground. (5) As the bus pulled up against the curb, dirty water splashed our feet.

(6) The driver's seat was on the opposite side of the bus, and the driver smiled at me when I showed him my ticket. (7) I looked out the window and realised that we were driving on the opposite side of the street. (8) All around us people who were on the wrong side of the street driving from what looked like the passenger seat. (9) The bus was filled with people. (10) Almost every seat was taken, and people were even standing in the aisle holding onto handrails and poles. (11) Their was a spiral staircase directly behind the driver, and we walked up to it to try to find more seats. (12) There were two rows of seats upstairs and a large window that looked onto the streets. (13) For seats were open near the front of the bus and we hurried to get them.

(14) The bus stopped every few seconds, and each time I had to hold onto my seat to keep from sliding into the aisle. (15) "What street are we looking for?" my dad asked my mom. (16) "Oxford" she replied. (17) I looked out the giant window. (18) We passed a large building that was shaped like an egg, and we continued to travel. (19) The bus driver's voice came over the speakers. (20) "Now approaching Liverpool," he said

(21) My mom looked at my dad. (22) I grabbed my sister's arm, but she was busy taking pictures of the buildings out the window. (23) "Liverpool," my mom whispered with a worried look on her face. (24) "We're lost, aren't we?" my dad said.

9. What change, if any, should be made in sentence 2?

a. Change *flew* to *flied*
b. Change *week* to *weak*
c. Change *sisters* to *sister's*
d. Make no change

10. What change, if any, should be made in sentence 7?

a. Change *realised* to *realize*
b. Change *street* to *streat*
c. Change *looked* to *look*
d. Make no change

11. What change, if any, should be made in sentence 11?

a. Delete the comma after *driver*
b. Change *Their* to *There*
c. Change *staircase* to *stair case*
d. Make no change

12. What change should be made in sentence 13?

a. Change *open* to *opened*
b. Change *were* to *was*
c. Change *For* to *Four*
d. Change *hurried* to *hurried*

13. Which of the following is the BEST way to rewrite the ideas in sentence 8?

a. All around us people were driving from what looked like the passenger seat, and they were driving on the opposite side of the street
b. All around us people who were on the wrong side of the street, driving from what looked like the passenger seat
c. All around us people were driving on the wrong side of the street. Driving from what looked like the passenger seat
d. All around us people were driving from what looked like passenger seat, they were on the opposite side of the street

14. What change, if any, should be made in sentence 16?

a. Change *Oxford* to *oxford*
b. Insert a comma after *Oxford*
c. Insert a period after the quotation mark
d. Make no change

15. Which sentence does not belong in this essay?

a. Sentence 20
b. Sentence 6
c. Sentence 13
d. Sentence 3

16. What is the BEST transition word or phrase that could be added to the beginning of sentence 19?

a. However
b. Once in a while
c. Additionally
d. After a while

Questions 17 -24 pertain to the following story:

Longhorn Café

(1) Last Saturday night my dad took me to watch the Longhorns play football in Austin. (2) It was a cool evening, and the orange-painted stadium was filled with screaming fans. (3) Even though we live in San Antonio, my dad has always been a dedicated Longhorns fan, and he wears his orange proudly.

(4) We arrived in Austin early. (5) "Traffic," my dad said as his only explanation. (6) He parked the truck down a small side street and motions for me to get out and follow him. (7) "I want to take you someplace," he said. (8) "I used to come here all the time when I was in college. (9) We walked up to a small building with a large patio off to the side. (10) A large tree with low branches spread across the patio and connected with the roof. (11) The leaves were beginning to change colors, and it was like sitting under a leafy canopy.

(12) We sat at a table outside on a rusting rocking bench beside an abandoned bathtub. (13) Stands of colored lights hung across the patio. (14) Wrapped around the tree. (15) "What is this place?" I asked. (16) My dad smiled and pointed to a sign bordered with colored lights. (17) "Spider Café," he said. (18) All around us, people were drinking coffee and staring at them computer screens. (19) Our waiter was named Chris, and he had a long beard, wore a dirtied apron, and carried empty coffee mugs.

(20) The waited came up to us, and my dad ordered himself a latte and a sweet drink for me. (21) My dad looked around the patio and smiled. (22) He leaned into the bench and placed his hand on the side of the bathtub. (23) He didn't even mind when he spilled coffee onto his favorite orange shirt. (24) "You'll love it here," he said, "when you are a Longhorn football player?"

17. What change, if any, should be made in sentence 5?

a. Delete the comma after *traffic*
b. Insert a comma after *said*
c. Change *said* to *says*
d. Make no change

18. What change should be made in sentence 6?

a. Change *parked* to *park*
b. Change *street* to *Street*
c. Insert a comma after *street*
d. Change *motions* to *motioned*

19. What change, if any, should be made in sentence 8?

a. Change *come* to *came*
b. Change *to* to *too*
c. Insert a quotation mark after *college*
d. Make no change

20. What revision, if any, is needed in sentences 13 and 14?

a. Strands of colored lights hung across the patio wrapped, around the tree
b. Strands of colored lights hung across the patio and wrapped around the tree
c. Strands of colored lights hung. Across the patio, wrapped around the tree
d. No revision is needed

21. What change, if any, should be made in sentence 18?

a. Change *them* to *their*
b. Delete the comma after *us*
c. Insert a comma after *and*
d. Make no change

22. Where is the best placement for sentence 19?

a. After sentence 22
b. After sentence 20
c. Before sentence 18
d. No change is needed

23. What change, if any, should be made in sentence 20?

a. Change *ordered* to *orders*
b. Change *himself* to *hisself*
c. Change *waited* to *waiter*
d. Make no change

24. What change should be made in sentence 24?

a. Change *Longhorn* to *longhorn*
b. Change *you are* to *your*
c. Change *football* to *Football*
d. Change the question mark to a period

Questions 25 – 32 pertain to the following story:

Strike Three

(1) As I stared down at the hitter in the batters box, I remembered what my dad had said to me. (2) "Shut everything out." (3) I focused on the glove in front of me. (4) I looked into the deep, blackened pocket, and sawed my target. (5) The batter tapped

his bat against the sides of his cleats, and rested the bat on his shoulders. (6) With hard eyes, he stares back at me.

(7) I kicked the front of my cleat into the bright white rubber on the pitching mound and took a deep breath. (8) Shut everything out," he had said. (9) Slowly the noises disappeared. (10) I could no longer hear the shouts from the parents in the stands. (11) In my head, I silenced the cheers from both dugouts. (12) The umpire did not exist. (13) There were no players, no coaches, not even a catcher. (14) There was just me. (15) The ball and the glove.

(16) I took a deep breath and brought my hands together at my chest. (17) I looked over at first base, but there was no runner. (18) In one motion, my feet left the rubber and connected with ground. (19) Dirt flew in the air as my arm rotated forward and released the ball in front of me. (20) I watched as the ball spun and landed into glove with a hard crack. (21) The umpire shot up from his crouched position and pointed his finger to the right and yelled, "Strike Three!"

(22) The noises came back. (23) The crowd cheered in the stands and I could here stomping feet. (24) My teammate clapped his hand to its glove and ran toward me. (25) My coach raised a first into the air in celebration. (26) I was surrounded by my teammates, and they were patting me on the back. (27) My dad was sitting on a bleacher behind home plate. (28) He raised his thumb to me and smiled as I ran off the field with my teammates.

25. What change, if any, should be made in sentence 1?

a. Change *stared* to *starred*
b. Change *dad* to *Dad*
c. Change *batters* to *batter's*
d. Make no change

26. What change should be made in sentence 4?

a. Change *blackened* to *blacked*
b. Change *sawed* to *saw*
c. Delete the comma after *deep*
d. Change *into* to *in to*

27. What change, if any, should be made in sentence 6?

a. Change *stares* to *stared.*
b. Change *me* to *I*
c. Delete the comma after *eyes*
d. Make no change

28. What change should be made in sentence 8?

a. Change *everything* to *every thing*
b. Delete the comma after *out*
c. Change the comma after *out* to a period
d. Insert quotation marks before *Shut*

29. What is the best way to combine sentence 14 and sentence 15?

a. There was just the ball, the glove, and me
b. There was just me, the ball, and the glove
c. There was just me and the ball and the glove
d. Make no change

30. What change, if any, should be made in sentence 23?

a. Change *cheered* to *cheer*
b. Change *here* to *hear*
c. Change *could* to *can*
d. Make no change

31. What sentence could BEST follow and support sentence 22?

a. My foot was still planted hard into the ground
b. The sounds came flooding into my ears as I looked up
c. I felt good
d. The umpire took off his mask and started walking toward the fence

32. What is the BEST transition word that could be added to the beginning of sentence 26?

a. However
b. Consequentially
c. Soon
d. Therefore

Questions 33 – 40 pertain to the following passage:

Imagine a Better World

(1) My favorite song is "imagine" by John Lennon. (2) It was released in 1971. (3) It is one of the few famous songs that John Lennon recorded and sang alone. (4) For the majority of his career, John Lennon was a member of an iconic rock band called the Beatles, a band that changed the music industry. (5) The Beatles accepted a lot of success in their career, with popular songs such as "I Want to Hold Your Hand," "Come Together," "Let it Be," and "Here Comes the Sun." (6) After the band decided to separate, John Lennon became a solo artist as well as an promoter for peace.

(7) "Imagine" tells the story of Lennons dream of peace in the world. He asks the listener to imagine different situations. (8) He says to imagine that there are no countries, religions, or possessions. (9) He says, "I wonder if you can." (10) This line strikes me the most I try to imagine such a world. (11) When talking about no possessions, he continues and says, "No need for greed or hunger." (12) It is a great line. (13) Throughout the song, he says, "Imagine all the people." (14) And he gives examples. (15) At first he says, "living for today," and then moves on to say, "living life in peace," and finally, "sharing all the world."

(16) My favorite part of the song is the chorus. (17) Lennon says, "You may say I'm a dreamer, but I'm not the only one. (18) I hope someday you'll join us, and the world will be as one." (19) When I really listen to the words of this song, I realize that "Imagine" is so much more than something that sounds nicely. (20) Lennon is saying something very important and suggesting ways in which the world can live in peace.

(21) Because of this song, I am a dreamer as well, and I join John Lennon in the fight for world peace.

33. What change, if any, should be made in sentence 1?

a. Change *favorite* to *favourite*
b. Change *imagine* to *Imagine*
c. Insert a comma after *song*
d. Make no change

34. What is the BEST verb to replace *accepted* in sentence 5?

a. Lasted
b. Liked
c. Had
d. Watched

35. What change should be made in sentence 6?

a. Change *separate* to *separated*
b. Insert a comma after *artist*
c. Change *solo* to *Solo*
d. Change *an* to *a*

36. What change, if any, should be made in sentence 7?

a. Change *Lennons* to *Lennon's*
b. Change *dream* to *dreamt*
c. Insert a comma after *peace*
d. Make no change

37. What is the BEST way to revise sentence 10?

a. This line strikes me the most as I try to imagine such a world.
b. This line strikes me the most, I try to imagine such a world.
c. This line strikes me, the most. I try to imagine such a world.
d. No revision needed.

38. What is the BEST way to combine sentence 13 and sentence 14?

a. Throughout the song, he says "Imagine all the people" and he gives examples.
b. Throughout the song, he says, "Imagine all the people," and he gives examples.
c. Throughout the song he says Imagine all the people, and he gives examples.
d. Throughout the song he says Imagine all the people and he gives examples.

39. What change, if any, should be made in sentence 18?

a. Insert a quotation mark before *I*
b. Move the period after the quotation marks
c. Change *you'll* to *youl'l*
d. Make no change

40. What change should be made in sentence 19?

a. Delete the comma after *song*
b. Change *something* to *some thing*
c. Change *nicely* to *nice*
d. Change *realize* to *realized*

Answer Key and Explanations

1. D: because this sentence is the simplest way to explain where Charlie was born. A is not correct because two sentences are not necessary. The additional subject and verb are unnecessary to express the idea. B is not correct, because *In a small town and on a farm* is a fragment. C is not correct, because the sentences contain awkward wording. The sentences need to be combined in order to express the idea in the simplest form.

2. A: because in this sentence, *crops* has been misspelled as *corps*. B is not correct, because the subject of the sentence, *mornings*, is plural. Therefore, the verb also must be plural for correct subject verb agreement. C is not correct, because this sentence does not need a comma.

3. B: because irregardless is not a word. The correct word is *regardless.* A is not correct because *complains* is in the present tense, while the rest of the paragraph is in the past tense. C is not correct, because a comma is needed after an introductory clause.

4. C: because this sentence supports both sentence 10 and sentence 11. The sentence supports the cause and effect idea that the attack on Pearl Harbor prompted the United States to become involved in the war, which caused Charlie to enlist in the army. A is not correct. Although this sentence provides new information, it does not link and support sentences 10 and 11. B is not correct. Although this sentence provides new information, it does not link and support sentences 10 and 11. D is not correct. Although this sentence provides new information, it does not link and support sentences 10 and 11.

5. A: because *European* is a proper noun and must be capitalized. B is not correct, because *becomes* is in the present tense, and the rest of the paragraph is written in the past tense. C is not correct, because a comma is not needed after *champion.*

6. B: because this sentence uses commas in a series as it lists aspects of Charlie's life after the war. Both *returned to Kentucky* and *married a woman named Bethany* are events that have happened and therefore need to be separated by a comma. A is not correct. *Returns* is in the present tense, and the rest of the paragraph is written in the past tense. C is not correct. The correct sentence uses commas in a series, and therefore only uses one *and* in the sentence.

7. D: because the sentence is correct as written. A is not correct. Although the rest of the essay is written in the past tense, the last paragraph begins with *Today* and is written in the present tense. Therefore, *loves* is correct. B is not correct, because this sentence does not need a comma. C is not correct. Both *beside* and *besides* are prepositions, but *beside* means "next to" and *besides* means "in addition to" or "other than." *Beside* is used in this sentence as "next to."

8. C: because in this sentence, *through* has been misspelled as *though*. A is not correct, because *colors* is spelled correctly. B is not correct, because this sentence needs a comma after *strawberries,* since the sentence contains a list and uses commas in a series.

9. C: In this sentence, *Sister's* is possessive and requires an apostrophe. A is not correct. *Flew* is the correct past tense of *fly*. B is not correct, because *week* is a noun and is spelled correctly.

10. A: because *realized* is misspelled in this sentence. B is not correct, because *street* is spelled correctly. C is not correct, because *look* is in the present tense, while the essay is written in past tense.

11. B: because a homonym has been misused. *There* is used to indicate a physical or abstract place, while *their* is used to indicate possession. A is not correct, because this sentence has two independent clauses joined by the conjunction *and*, and a comma is used before the conjunction. C is not correct, because *staircase* is one word.

12. C: because a homonym has been misused. *Four* is a number. A is not correct, because in this sentence *open* is used as a noun rather than a verb and does not need to be in the past tense. B is not correct. *Were* is plural, and *was* is singular. The subject of the sentence, *seats*, is plural; therefore, the verb also must be plural for correct subject verb agreement. D is not correct, because *hurried* is spelled correctly.

13. A: because this rewording of this sentence makes the meaning clear and is grammatically correct. B is not correct because this sentence is a fragment. C is not correct because the second sentence is a fragment. D is not correct because this sentence is a run-on sentence.

14. B: because a comma is needed before the closing quotation when the sentence is not completed with the quotation. A is not correct because *Oxford* is a proper noun and must be capitalized. C is not correct. The sentence does not end with the quotation; therefore, a comma, rather than a period, goes before the quotation mark.

15. D: because this sentence this sentence provides new information that is not important to the rest of the essay. Answers A, B, and C are incorrect, because all of these sentences present content that is important to the essay.

16. D: In the previous sentence, the phrase *we continued to travel*, suggests a passage of time. A proper transition into the next sentence would involve the acknowledgement that time has passed. A is not correct because *however* is not a good transition into the sentence. B is not correct. Although *once in a while* relates to time, it does not transition well into the sentence given the context of the previous sentence. C is not correct. *Additionally* is not a good transition into the sentence because it does not indicate a passage of time.

17. D: because the sentence is correct as written. A is not correct, because a comma is needed before the closing quotation when the sentence is not completed with the quotation. B is not correct because this sentence does not need a comma. C is not correct because *says* is in the present tense, and the essay is written in the past tense.

18. D: because *motions* is in the present tense, and the rest of the essay is written in the past tense. B is not correct because *street* is not used in this sentence as a proper noun and does not need to be capitalized. C is not correct. A comma is unnecessary because the second sentence is not an independent clause.

19. C: because a quotation mark is needed to end dialogue. A is incorrect because *come* is in the present tense, and the essay is written in the past tense. B is not correct. *Too* means "also" or an indication of excess.

20. B: because this sentence is grammatically correct as written. A is not correct. The comma is misplaced and disrupts the sentence. C is not correct because the second sentence is a fragment. D is not correct because sentence 14 is a fragment.

21. A: because *their* indicates possession; *them* does not. *Computer screens* belong to the subject, *people*. B is not correct. *All around us* is an introductory clause and needs a comma. C is not correct.

Staring at them computer screens is not an independent clause and therefore does not need a comma.

22. B: because the sentence provides additional information about the waiter. The sentence should be placed after the waiter has been introduced in sentence 20. A is not correct. The subject of the paragraph has shifted to the father at sentence 21, and therefore a sentence involving information about the waiter would be out of place after sentence 22. C is not correct. Sentence 18 provides setting information. A sentence involving information about the waiter before this sentence would be out of place. D is not correct. This sentence provides additional information about the waiter and should not conclude a paragraph.

23. C: because *waiter* has been misspelled. A is not correct. *Orders* is in the present tense, and the essay is written in the past tense. B is not correct because *himself* is the correct word, while *hisself* is not a word.

24. D: because the sentence is a statement, not a question. Therefore, the sentence needs to be punctuated with a period. A is not correct. In this sentence, *longhorn* refers to the mascot of a sports team and is a proper noun. Proper nouns need to be capitalized. B is not correct. *You* and *are* in this sentence are used as both a subject and a verb. *Your* indicates possession. C is not correct. *Football* is not a proper noun and does not require capitalization.

25. C: In this sentence, *batter's* is possessive and needs an apostrophe. A is not correct because *stared*, the past tense of the verb, *stare*, is spelled correctly. B is not correct. In this sentence, *dad* is not a proper noun, since it is not used as a name. *My* before *dad* indicates that it is not a proper noun.

26. B: because *saw* is the correct past tense of the verb, *see*. A is not correct because *blackened* is the correct adjective. C is not correct. A comma is needed to separate adjectives when each adjective separately describes the noun. D is not correct. *Into* is spelled correctly.

27. A: because *stares* is in the present tense, and the rest of the essay is in the past tense. *Stared* is the correct past tense of *stare*. B is not correct. *Me* is the object of the sentence because it is the recipient of the action, *stares*. I is traditionally used as a subject. C is not correct. *With hard eyes* is an introductory clause, and a comma is needed after the clause.

28. D: It is correct because the quotation marks after *out* indicate dialogue. Quotation marks are needed before *Shut* to begin the dialogue. A is not correct. When used as a noun, *everything* is one word. B is not correct. A comma is needed before the closing quotation when the sentence is not completed with the quotation. C is not correct. The sentence is not completed with the quotation, and therefore it needs a comma rather than a period before the closing quotation.

29. A: because this sentence is grammatically correct. B is not correct. When using the pronoun, *me*, in a series, it is always placed at the end of the series. C is not correct. The repetition of *and* is not grammatically correct. The nouns need to be separated using commas in a series.

30. B: It is correct because a homonym has been misused. *Hear* indicates the act of hearing and listening. *Here* indicates location. A is not correct. *Cheer* is in the present tense, and the rest of the essay is in the past tense. C is not correct. *Can* is in the present tense, and the rest of the essay is in the past tense.

31. B: It is correct because this sentence supports both sentence 22 and 23. The preceding sentence discusses noises coming back. The next logical sentence should have something to do with noises. A is not correct. Although this sentence provides new information, it does not link and support sentences 22 and 23. C is not correct. Although this sentence provides new information, it does not link and support sentences 22 and 23. D is not correct. Although this sentence provides new information, it does not link and support sentences 22 and 23.

32. C: because a proper transition into the next sentence would involve the acknowledgement that time has passed. A is not correct. *However* is not a good transition into this sentence since it does not require a shift in ideas. B is not correct. *Consequentially* is not a good transition into this sentence since it presents no cause and effect. D is not correct. *Therefore* is not a good transition into this sentence since it presents no cause and effect.

33. B: because *imagine* is a proper noun. As the title of a song, it requires capitalization. A is not correct. *Favorite* is spelled correctly. C is not correct. *My favorite song* is not an introductory clause, so a comma is not needed.

34. C: The missing verb in this sentence must have something to do with possession since it discusses the band's success. *Had* indicates possession. A, B, and D are incorrect, because these verbs do not fit within the sentence.

35. D: It is correct because in the sentence, the article *an* is followed by a noun, *promoter. Promoter* begins with a consonant and a consonant sound and therefore must be followed by the article *a.* A is not correct. The verb in this sentence is *decided,* not *separate,* and therefore *separate* does not need to be in the past tense like the rest of the paragraph. B is not correct because the comma is unnecessary. C is not correct. *Solo* is not a proper noun and does not need to be capitalized.

36. A: because *Lennon* is possessive in this sentence; therefore, it requires an apostrophe. B is not correct. In this sentence, *dream* is a noun rather than a verb, so it does not need to be in the past tense. C is not correct, because a comma is unnecessary.

37. A: because the sentence is missing the article *as.* This is the simplest way to express the idea of the sentence. B is incorrect because this sentence is not grammatically correct. C is incorrect because the first sentence is grammatically incorrect.

38. B: This is the simplest way to express the idea in a grammatically correct sentence. F is incorrect because a comma is missing after *song* and after *people.* H is incorrect because a comma is missing after *song,* and quotation marks are missing around the quotation, *"Imagine all the people."* J is not correct. A comma is missing after *song* and after *people,* and quotation marks are missing around the quotation, *"Imagine all the people."*

39. D: It is correct because the sentence is correct. A is not correct. This sentence is part of a longer quotation that began in the previous sentence. Since the quotation is continuing, the sentence does not begin with quotation marks. B is not correct. In a quotation, the punctuation is placed before the ending quotation marks. C is not correct. *You'll* is the correct contraction of *you will.*

40. C: In this sentence nice is an adjective rather than an adverb. It describes the noun, *sounds,* not the verb. A is not correct. *When I really listen to the words of this song* is an introductory clause, and a comma is needed after the clause. B is not correct. *Something* is one word when used as a noun. D is not correct. Although most of the essay is in the past tense, the final paragraph is in the present tense. *Realized* is in the past tense.

Sample Composition

Write a composition about a time when you made a hard decision.

Last November, I was sitting in my third period math class when my teacher told me that she needed to talk to me after class. I was worried that I had done something wrong or had forgotten to turn in a homework assignment. I thought about it, but could not remember missing any assignments. I also thought that maybe I had failed the last test, but I felt that I had done well on it. When I finally talked to her, I was relieved to hear that she wanted to move me up into the accelerated math class. I immediately thought of my friend, Alex. He and I were in the same math class, and it was the only class we had together. I wanted to be in accelerated math, but I did not want to leave my friend.

When I came home from school, I told my parents what my teacher had said. "Wow!" my mom said, "That is great!" My dad smiled at me. "Good job," he said. "I am really proud of you." It made me happy to know that my parents were proud and excited for me. I was excited too, but I was also scared. I decided to talk to my mom about it. I told her that I did not want to leave class with Alex because we had no other classes together and that I was afraid. "What are you afraid of?" she asked. I told her that I was already behind in the accelerated math class, and that I was afraid I would not be able to catch up. I was also afraid that the class would be too hard for me.

"Well, that's a lot to think about," my mom said. She told me to look at everything I was afraid of and think about each thing. She said I needed a plan. She told me that if my teacher thought I could do well in the accelerated class, I should listen to her and believe in myself. I told her I thought that I could spend extra time with the new teacher learning the material that I had missed. "But what about Alex?" I said. I still did not want to leave my friend. "You always have recess," she said.

I decided to join the accelerated math class and am very happy. It was hard at first to keep up with the work that I had missed, but I like learning new things. I have made a lot of new friends, but I also see Alex at recess. We all have fun. The accelerated math class was better for me, and I am happy I made this hard decision.

Practice Test #2

Questions 1 – 8 pertain to the following story:

The Greek Festival

(1) Every October my family attends the Greek Festival at the Greek Orthodox Church close to our house. (2) We were first invited four years ago by one of my friends, Amelia. (3) Her family attends the Greek Orthodox Church and works several booths at the festival each year. (4) They telled us that everyone was welcome.

(5) When we first arrived at the festival, we could hear the music from the parking lot? (6) It was music that I had never heard before, and some of it was in another language. (7) Amelia told me later that it was traditional Greek music. (8) We also noticed the smells that seemed to come from all over the festival grounds. (9) All around us, there were signs for meat, pastry, coffee drinks, and other side dishes. (10) My mom's favorite were the grape leaves, and my dad loved the Baklava. (11) It is a dessert is made up baked thin sheets of pastry dough covered in a sweet sauce like honey. (12) Amelia suggested us eat it with ice cream and chocolate sauce. (13) As much as I liked the baklava, my favorite was the gyro pita. (14) Gyro is lamb meat in a warm pita with tomato, lettuce, onion, and a Greek sauce. (15) I ate two pitas and it was deliciously!

(16) After we had eaten, everyone gathered around the dance floor and watched as people from all different age groups danced traditional Greek dances. (17) The dancers were dressed in special clothing and black dress shoes.

(18) Amelia danced in the second group of dancers, and her mom tossed money toward her. (19) Soon, the dance floor was covered in dollar bills from all of the dancers families. (20) The food was great, the music was fun, and the dancing was even better. (21) We had a great time at the greek Festival, and now I look forward to it every year!

1. What change, if any, should be made in sentence 4?

a. Change everyone to every one
b. Change telled to told
c. Change welcome to welcomed
d. Make no change

2. What change should be made in sentence 5?

a. Change arrived to arrive
b. Change festival to Festival
c. Delete the comma after festival
d. Change the question mark to a period

3. What change, if any, should be made in sentence 10?

a. Change were to was
b. Change mom's to moms
c. Change loved to loves
d. Make no change

4. What revision, if any, is needed in sentence 11?

a. It is a dessert that is made up of baked thin sheets of pastry dough covered in a sweet sauce like honey.
b. It is a dessert, is made up baked thin sheets of pastry dough covered in a sweet sauce like honey.
c. It is a dessert. Made up baked thin sheets of pastry dough covered in a sweet sauce like honey.
d. No revision needed.

5. What is the BEST way to revise sentence 12?

a. Amelia suggested, us eat it with ice cream and chocolate sauce.
b. Amelia suggested to us eat it with ice cream and chocolate sauce.
c. Amelia suggested us eat it, with ice cream and chocolate sauce.
d. Amelia suggested that we eat it with ice cream and chocolate sauce.

6. What change, if any, should be made in sentence 15?

a. Change ate to eat
b. Change deliciously to delicious
c. Change two to too
d. Make no change

7. What change, if any, should be made in sentence 19?

a. Change covered to cover
b. Change from to form
c. Change dancers to dancers'
d. Make no change

8. What change, if any, should be made in sentence 21?

a. Change had to have
b. Change look to looked
c. Change greek to Greek
d. Make no change

Questions 9 – 16 pertain to the following passage:

Dogs in the Park

(1) On Saturday, my mom took me to a dog show at a park by our house. (2) The sun was out, and it was a really warm day. (3) I ride my bike to the park almost every day in the summer. (4) The dogs were all lying in the grass when we arrived, and they looked warm in the sun. (5) One of my mom's friends Mary, is a dog trainer, and she invited us to watch the dog show after my mom told her how much I love dogs.

(6) Their were all kinds of dogs at the show. (7) Some were really little, some were big, and some had really long hair. (8) My favorite were the dogs in the toy category and the sporting category. (9) The dogs that were waiting to be shown were with their trainers at different areas of the park getting ready. (10) Some trainers brushed its dog's hair, and some gave treats.

(11) We sat on the grass and watched the show. (12) The trainers were all dressed up. (13) The men wore suit pants and jackets, and the women wore dress skirts, stockings, and blazers. (14) All of the dogs were lined up and stood still wile the judges walked down and looked closely at all the dogs. (15) The judges looked at the dogs' hair, paws, and teeth. (16) Then it was time for each dog to show off. (17) Each trainer ran with their dog and held the leash high in the air. (18) The judges watched as the dogs ran, and judged how good they turned corners and listened to their trainers.

(19) At the end of the show, the judges awarded prizes. (20) The dogs and their trainers gathered in a line, and the judges presnted the winners with large ribbons. (21) Mary's dog won first place, and she was given a purple ribbon that was bigger than most of the small dogs in the toy category. (22) We left the park, and I told my mom that I want to learn how to train dogs.

9. What change should be made in sentence 5?

a. Change is to was
b. Delete the comma after Mary
c. Change invited to invites
d. Insert a comma after friends

10. What change, if any, should be made in sentence 6?

a. Change Their to There
b. Change dogs to dog's
c. Change were to was
d. Make no change

11. What change, if any, should be made in sentence 8?

a. Change were to was
b. Insert a comma after category
c. Change favorite to favorites
d. Make no change

12. What change should be made in sentence 10?

a. Change its to their
b. Change its to it's
c. Change brushed to brush
d. Change dog's to dogs

13. What change should be made in sentence 14?

a. Insert a comma after up
b. Change walked to walk
c. Change wile to while
d. Insert a comma after down

14. What change, if any, should be made in sentence 20?

a. Change dogs to dog
b. Change presented to preseented
c. Change their to its
d. Make no change

15. Which sentence does not belong in this essay?

a. Sentence 18
b. Sentence 11
c. Sentence 7
d. Sentence 3

16. What is the BEST transition word that could be added to the beginning of sentence 22?

a. However
b. Later
c. Otherwise
d. Consequentially

Questions 17 – 24 pertain to the following story:

First Party

(1) Today my brother turned one year old. (2) We had a big party to celebrate, and a lot of people came. (3) My ant came to the house early to help my mom hang streamers. (4) My cousin helped me make party favors for both the big kids and the babies. (5) We packed the little bags with candy, pencils, whistles, and noisemakers. (6) My parents invited a lot of people. (7) Soon the house was filled with family, friends, and even some babies for my brother to play with.

(8) My grandparents on my dad's side flew even flew in from California the day before to help. (9) My dad lighted the barbeque in the back yard and took orders from the guests. (10) He made hamburgers, turkey burgers, hot dogs, chicken wings, and sausages. (11) My aunt sliced strips of onion, tomato, pickles, and lettuce. (12) She also cuts up an avocado because she knows that it is my favorite topping on my hamburger. (13) My cousins, friends, and I all played in the backyard after we ate.

(14) My brother slept through most of the party, he was awake by the time he had cake. (15) He don't know he was missing his party by napping. (16) My mom put him in his high chair, and we all sang "Happy birthday," to him. (17) There was one candle in the center of the large cake, and my mom blew it out since he was two little.

(18) My brother sat in his chair and ate cake. (19) Soon there was cake everywhere. (20) It was all over his hands, his face, his tabletop and chair. (21) There was blue icing everywhere. (22) He even lifted up his arms and grabbed pieces of his hair. (23) His big, blue eyes looked at everyone as they smiled and laughed. (24) He stuffed some more cake into his mouth and smiled. (25) I think he knew he had a good first birthday.

17. What change should be made in sentence 3?

a. Change hang to hanged
b. Change ant to aunt
c. Change help to helped
d. Change came to comes

18. Where is the best placement for sentence 8?

a. After sentence 2
b. After sentence 4
c. After sentence 5
d. No change is needed

19. What change, if any, should be made in sentence 9?

a. Change took to takes
b. Change barbeque to BBQ
c. Change lighted to lit
d. Make no change

20. What change, if any, should be made in sentence 12?

a. Change know to knew
b. Change cuts to cut
c. Change an to a
d. Make no change

21. What is the BEST transition word that could be added to the beginning of sentence 14?

a. Later
b. Therefore
c. Although
d. However

22. What change, if any, should be made in sentence 15?

a. Change don't to didn't
b. Change was to is
c. Change napping to nap
d. Make no change

23. What change should be made in sentence 16?

a. Change his to him
b. Change put to puts
c. Delete the quotation marks
d. Change birthday to Birthday

24. What change should be made in sentence 17?

a. Change There to They're
b. Delete the comma before and
c. Change blew to blowed
d. Change two to too

Questions 25 – 32 pertain to the passage:

Dinner is Served

(1) Every year my friend and I celebrate each other's birthdays by going out to dinner because our birthdays are three weeks apart. (2) On my birthday, my family took us to Aribba, my favorite mexican food restaurant. (3) For Annmae's birthday, she chose a Japanese restaurant called Tomo where the food is cooked at the table.

(4) I had never eaten Japanese food before and didn't know what to expect? (5) When the hostess brought us to our table, I was surprised to see that there were four extra seats. (6) That was not the only thing that was strange. (7) The table was not a regular restaurant dinner table. (8) It was a half circle and there was a giant sheet of metal in the center. (9) The hostess came back with other people and sat them with us at our table.

(10) We filled out cards that said what kind of food we wanted. (11) We had to pick between chicken, beef, shrimp, and pork. (12) A man then came to our table and lit the metal sheet. (13) He laid out rice and vegetables, and started cutting and cooking. (14) He worked very fast it was almost hard for me to see his hands. (15) After the rice, he cooked each of the different meats and started serving plates. (16) While things were cooking he would take his spatula and fling a piece of bell pepper or carrot at someone at the table. (17) He toss the most at Annmae since it was her birthday, but they all hit her chin and slid down onto her shirt.

(18) It was really exciting watching our food cooked right in front of us. (19) The chef was nice and the food is delicious. (20) I even liked having other people sit at our table because it was like being at a party at dinner. (21) I am really glad that my friend chose Tomo and I can't wait to see where we try next year!

25. What change, if any, should be made in sentence 2?

a. Change birthday to birth day
b. Delete the comma after birthday
c. Change mexican to Mexican
d. Make no change

26. What change should be made in sentence 4?

a. Change had to have
b. Change Japanese to japanese
c. Change didn't to don't
d. Change the question mark to a period

27. What sentence could BEST follow and support sentence 9?

a. Now I understood why there were extra seats
b. The hostess smiled at us as she left
c. The woman worse a blue dress and he hair was tied back
d. I wondered how many times she was going to come back

28. What change, if any, should be made in sentence 10?

a. Change filled to filed
b. Change said to says
c. Change wanted to want
d. Make no change

29. What is the BEST way to revise sentence 14?

a. He worked very fast it was almost hard for me, to see his hands.
b. He worked very fast, and it was almost hard for me to see his hands.
c. His hands worked very fast it was almost hard for me to see.
d. Make no revision.

30. What change, if any, should be made in sentence 16?

a. Change were to are
b. Insert a comma after cooking
c. Change take to took
d. Make no change

31. What change, if any, should be made in sentence 17?

a. Delete the comma after birthday
b. Change hit to hitted
c. Change toss to tossed
d. Make no change

32. What change should be made in sentence 19?

a. Change is to was
b. Change was to is
c. Change delicious to deliciously
d. Change chef to Chef

Questions 33 – 40 pertain to the following passage:

History's Unsinkable Lessons

(1) In Ruth Campbell's book Exploring the Titanic, the events of the famous ship's only journey and sinking are brought to life. (2) In 1912, Titanic was built and was the largest passenger steamship at the time. (3) On what would be its first and only journey, the ship departed from Southampton in England and was supposed to arrive in New York City. (4) The ship hit an iceberg late at night on April 14, 1912, and sunked less than three hours later.

(5) Titanic was designed by some of the best engineers and had the latest technology of the time. (6) The ship was made to carry over three and a half thousand passengers and crew members, but had only twenty lifeboats. (7) There was not enough lifeboats for all of the people onboard, and as a result, only seven hundred six people survived.

(8) One interesting thing about Titanic, is that the ship was divided into classes. (9) The most expensive tickets were first class, and first class passengers had the biggest and much luxurious rooms. (10) The first class rooms were the closest to the ship's deck. (11) Because this the majority of survivors came from first class. (12) They were able to reach the deck fastest to get a seat on a lifeboat. (13) The third class rooms

were located the farthest below deck, and the majority of the third class passengers did not survive.

(14) Ruth Campbell's book was very interesting but also sad because the story of Titanic is true. (15) However, Campbell ended the book by talking about the positive things that have happened because of this tragedy. (16) Most importantly, experts now recommend that ships' carry enough lifeboats for all passengers onboard. (17) This would have saved a lot of lifes. (18) It was a good book, and it displayed a good message in history that lessons should be learned from mistakes.

33. What change should be made in sentence 1?

a. Change ship's to ships
b. Insert a comma after book
c. Change are to is
d. Change brought to bring

34. What change, if any, should be made in sentence 4?

a. Change sunked to sank
b. Delete the comma after 14
c. Change hours to hour's
d. Make no change

35. What change should be made in sentence 7?

a. Change There to They're
b. Delete the comma after onboard
c. Change lifeboats to lifeboats'
d. Change was to were

36. What change, if any, should be made in sentence 8?

a. Change was to were
b. Delete the comma after Titanic
c. Change divided into divide
d. Make no change

37. What is the BEST way to revise and combine sentence 11 and sentence 12?

a. Because, the majority of survivors came from first class as they were able to reach the deck fastest to get a seat on a lifeboat
b. Because of this, the majority of survivors came from first class, as they were able to reach the deck fastest to get a seat on a lifeboat
c. Because this, the majority of survivors came from first class, they were able to reach the deck fastest to get a seat on a lifeboat
d. Because of this, the majority of survivors came from first class as they were able to reach the deck fastest to get a seat on a lifeboat

38. What is the BEST transition that could be added to the beginning of sentence 13?

a. Lastly
b. For example
c. On the other hand
d. Therefore

39. What change should be made in sentence 16?

a. Change most important to importantist
b. Change found to find
c. Insert a comma after important
d. Change ship's to ships

40. What change, if any, should be made in sentence 17?

a. Change would have to would
b. Change a lot to a lot
c. Change lifes to lives
d. Make no change

Answer Key and Explanations

1. B: because told is the correct past tense of the verb tell. Telled is not a word. A is not correct. When used as a noun, everyone is one word. C is not correct. Welcome is not a verb in this sentence and therefore does not need to be in the past tense like the rest of the essay.

2. D: because this sentence is a statement rather than a question. As a result, it should be punctuated with a period and not a question mark. A is not correct. Arrive is in the present tense, and the rest of the paragraph is in the past tense. B is not correct. Festival is not used in this sentence as a proper noun and therefore does not need to be capitalized. C is not correct. When we first arrived at the festival is an introductory clause, and a comma is needed after the introductory clause.

3. A: because the subject of this sentence is favorite. Favorite is singular; therefore, the verb also must be singular in order for the subject and verb to agree. Were is plural. Was is singular. B is not correct. Mom's in this sentence is possessive and an apostrophe is needed. C is not correct. Loves is in the present tense, and the rest of the essay is in the past tense.

4. A: This is the simplest way to express the idea in a grammatically correct sentence. B is not correct, because this sentence is not grammatically correct. C is not correct, because the second sentence is a fragment.

5. D: because it is the simplest way to express the idea in a grammatically correct sentence. A, B, and C are incorrect because these sentences are not grammatically correct. This sentence is not grammatically correct.

6. B: because deliciously is an adverb rather than an adjective. It describes the noun, pitas, not the verb. A is not correct. Eat is in the present tense, and the rest of the essay is in the past tense. C is not correct. Two is spelled correctly and indicates the number. Too means "as well" or an indication of excess.

7. C: because in this sentence dancers' is possessive and needs an apostrophe. Since dancers is plural, referring to more than one dancer, the apostrophe comes after the s. A is not correct. Cover is in the present tense, and the rest of the essay is in the past tense. B is not correct. The correct word is from, and it is spelled correctly.

8. C: It is correct because Greek is a proper noun and needs to be capitalized. A is not correct. Have is in the present tense, and the rest of the essay is in the past tense. B is not correct. A shift has occurred in the last sentence, and the second half of the sentence shifts into the present tense. The writer explains that she looks forward to the festival every year. Look in the present tense is therefore correct.

9. D: It is correct because a comma is needed to separate the interjection of the name. A is not correct. Even though is is in the present tense and the rest of the essay is in the past tense, the sentence is describing a current person and should be in the present tense. B is not correct. A comma is needed to separate the interjection of the name. C is not correct. Invites is in the present tense and the rest of the essay, as a past event, is in the past tense.

10. A: It is correct because a homonym has been misused. There is used to indicate a physical or abstract place. Their is used to indicate possession. B is not correct. In this sentence, dogs does not indicate possession and does not need an apostrophe. C is not correct. Was is in the present tense, and the rest of the essay is in the past tense.

11. C: It is correct because the verb in the sentence, were, is plural, and the subject must be plural for subject-verb agreement. A is not correct. Was is in the present tense, and the rest of the essay is in the past tense. B is not correct. A comma is not needed because and the sporting category is not an independent clause.

12. A: It is correct because there is plural and displays possession. Its is singular. The subject, trainers, is plural; therefore, the possession is plural as well. B is not correct. It's is only used as a contraction for it is, not for possession. C is not correct. Brush is in the present tense, and the rest of the essay is in the past tense. D is not correct. Dog's is possessive and needs an apostrophe.

13. C: It is correct because a homonym has been misused. Wile means to trick or fool, and while indicates a period of time. A is not correct. A comma is not needed. No introductory clause or independent clauses need to be joined by a comma and conjunction. B is not correct. Walk is in the present tense and the rest of the essay is in the past tense. D is not correct. A comma is not needed. An independent clause does not follow the conjunction.

14. B: It is correct because presented has been misspelled. A is not correct. Their trainers indicates that dogs should be plural, not singular. C is not correct. Their is plural and its is singular. The subject, dogs, is plural.

15. D: It is correct because although this sentence provides new information, the content is not important to the rest of the essay. A, B, and C are because these sentences are important to the essay.

16. B: It is correct because the opening phrase, We left the park, indicates a time lapse from the earlier events of the essay. An appropriate transition word would indicate time. A is not correct. However is not a good transition because sentence 22 is not contradicting anything in the previous sentence. C is not correct. Otherwise is not a good transition because sentence 22 does not suggest an alternate to something that occurred previously. D is not correct. Consequentially is not a good transition because the content of the sentence is not cause and effect from the previous sentence.

17. B: It is correct because a homonym has been misused. Ant refers to an insect, and aunt refers to the sister of one's mother. A is not correct. Hang is not the verb of this sentence and does not need to be in the past tense. C is not correct. Help is not the verb of this sentence and does not need to be in the past tense. D is not correct. Came is the verb of this sentence. Comes is in the present tense and the rest of the essay is in the past tense.

18. A: It is correct because the sentence discusses the grandparents traveling from California to help with the part. Therefore, this sentence should be placed after the description of the party and that a lot of people came. B is not correct. Sentence 4 discusses the cousin helping with party favors, and therefore a sentence about the grandparents' travel would not follow well.

C is not correct. Sentence 5 discusses the party favors, and therefore a sentence about the grandparents' travel would not follow well.

19. C: It is correct because lit is the correct past tense for the verb light. A is not correct. Takes is in the present tense and the rest of the essay is in the past tense. B is not correct. Barbeque is spelled correctly. BBQ is an abbreviation, not a word.

20. B: It is correct because cuts is in the present tense, and the rest of the essay is in the past tense. Cut is in the past tense. A is not correct. Even though the essay is in the past tense, the act of the aunt knowing is a present and ongoing action and should be in the present tense. C is not correct. In this sentence, the article an is followed by a noun, avocado. Avocado begins with a vowel and a vowel sound; therefore, it needs to be introduced with the article an.

21. C: It is correct because although means "in spite of" and is appropriate within the sentence. A is not correct. Later is not an appropriate transition word because it contradicts the beginning of the sentence. B is not correct. Therefore is not an appropriate transition word because there is no cause an effect from the previous sentence. D is not correct. However is not an appropriate transition word because sentence 14 does not contradict anything from the previous sentence.

22. A: It is correct because don't is the conjunction of do not. Do not is in the present tense, and the rest of the essay is in the past tense. The past tense of do is did. B is not correct. Is is in the present tense, and the rest of the essay is in the past tense. C is not correct. Napping is a verb in this sentence, not a noun.

23. D: It is correct because birthday is used as part of a song title. Song titles are proper nouns and need to be capitalized. A is not correct. His in this sentence indicates possession; him does not. B is not correct. Puts is in the present tense, and the rest of the essay is in the past tense. C is not correct. Quotations are needed around song titles.

24. D: It is correct because a homonym has been misused. Two is the number. Too indicates "also," "excessively," or "very." A is not correct. There indicates location. They're is the contraction of there are. B is not correct. The sentence has two independent clauses joined by the conjunction and. A comma needs to be before the conjunction. H is not correct. Blew is the correct past tense of blow. Blowed is not a word.

25. C: It is correct because Mexican is a proper noun, and proper nouns need to be capitalized. A is not correct. Birthday is one word. B is not correct. A comma is needed after an introductory clause.

26. D: It is correct because the sentence is a statement, not a question, and needs a period as punctuation. A is not correct. Have is in the present tense, and the rest of the essay is in the past tense. B is not correct. Japanese is a proper noun and needs to be capitalized. C is not correct. Didn't is a contraction of did not and is in the past tense, like the rest of the essay. Don't is a contraction of do not and is in the present tense.

27. A: It is correct because the sentence both supports the previous sentences and provides additional information. Sentence 5 states that extra seats were available at the table. This sentence provides additional information that supports sentence 5 as well as sentence 9. B, C, and D are incorrect. Although these sentences provide new information, they do not link and support the previous sentences.

28. D: It is correct because this sentence is grammatically correct. A is not correct. Within the context of the sentence, a card is filled out, not filed out. B is not correct. Says is in the present tense, and the rest of the essay is in the past tense. C is not correct. Want is in the present tense, and the rest of the essay is in the past tense.

29. B: It is correct because it is the simplest way to express the idea in a grammatically correct sentence. A and C are not correct because these sentences are not grammatically correct.

30. B: It is correct because While things were cooking is an introductory clause, and a comma is needed after the clause. A is not correct. Are is in the present tense and the rest of the essay is in the past tense. C is not correct. Take is part of would take and is in the past participle, not the present tense.

31. C: It is correct because tossed is in the past tense, like the rest of the essay. Toss is in the present tense. A is not correct. A comma is needed before the conjunction when two independent clauses are joined by a conjunction. B is not correct. Hit is the correct past tense of hit. Hitted is not a word.

32. A: It is correct because was is in the past tense, like the rest of the essay. Is is in the present tense. B is not correct. Is is in the present tense and the rest of the essay is in the past tense. C is not correct. Delicious is an adjective, not an adverb. It is used in this sentence to describe the noun, not the verb. D is not correct. Chef is not a proper noun and does not need to be capitalized.

33. B: It is correct because a comma is needed to separate the interjection of the book title. A is not correct. Ship in the sentence is possessive and requires the apostrophe. C is not correct. Are is the plural of is. The subject, events, is plural and therefore the verb needs to be plural in subject-verb agreement. D is not correct. Are brought is in the past participle, and bring is in the present tense.

34. A: It is correct because sank is the correct past tense of the verb sink. Sunked is not a word. B is not correct. A comma is needed to separate dates of the month from the year. H is not correct. Hours is not possessive and does not require the apostrophe.

35. D: It is correct because were is the plural past tense of is. The subject of the sentence, lifeboats, is plural, and the verb also must be plural in subject-verb agreement. A is not correct. There is used correctly. They're is a contraction of they are. B is not correct. A comma is needed to separate the interjection, and as a result. C is not correct. Lifeboats is not possessive and does not require the apostrophe.

36. B: It is correct because there is no need for a comma. As it stands, the comma disrupts the normal flow of thought in the sentence. A is not correct. The subject, ship, is singular, and the verb also must be singular in subject-verb agreement. C is not correct. Was divided is in the past participle. Divide is in the present tense, and the rest of the essay is in the past.

37. B: It is correct because it is the simplest way to express the idea in a grammatically correct sentence. Because of this refers to the content of the previous sentence. A is not correct. This sentence is not grammatically correct. C is not correct. This sentence is not grammatically correct. D is not correct. This sentence is not grammatically correct and needs a comma after class.

38. C: Choice C shows the contrast between first-class and third-class passengers. The previous sentences explained why majority of the survivors were a part of the first class passengers. Sentence 13 shifts to explain explains why most of the third class passengers did not survive. "On the other hand" clearly signals this contrast. "Lastly" is not an appropriate transition word, as there was not a series of listed facts. "For example" is not an appropriate transition to use since it is not giving an example. "Therefore" is not an appropriate transition word because the new information does not involve cause and effect with the previous sentences.

39. D: because in this sentence, ships is plural rather than possessive and does not require the apostrophe. A is not correct. Most important is correct. Importantist is not a word. B is not correct. Find is in the present tense and the rest of the essay is in the past tense. C is not correct, because the sentence does not need a comma. A comma would disrupt the normal flow of thought in the sentence.

40. C: It is correct because lives is the correct plural of life. Lifes is not a word. A is not correct. Would have is in the past participle, and would is in the future tense. B is not correct. A lot is correct. Alot is not a word

Sample Composition

Write a composition about a time in your life when you learned an important lesson.

It is a tradition in my family that we all go shopping for Thanksgiving together. Every year we buy two of everything. We buy two turkeys, two bags of potatoes, two pies, and lots of canned foods. My mom says it is important for us to go shopping as a family and really think about what we are buying. At the end of the shopping trip, we take half of the food, put it away in the house, and leave the other half in the car. Then we all get back into the car and Dad drives us to the homeless shelter. We give the shelter the rest of the food.

I did not want to go to the homeless shelter when I was younger. I wanted to stay at home and watch cartoons. I did not even want to go shopping for the food. I thought it was boring and that I had better things to do. My mom told me that I had to go and that it was very important. I remember my mom looking at the turkeys. She bought two of them. One was medium sized, and one was so big that she needed help putting it into the cart. "Go pick out some potatoes," she said to me. "And some green beans." I looked for a really long time to get the best green beans and potatoes for the shelter. It was fun to try to find the best.

When we got to the homeless shelter, people were lined up for over a block. They were all standing and wrapped in old blankets. I didn't understand. I asked my mom why they were lined up and why they were standing in the cold. She said that they did not live in a house like me and that they were lined up to get dinner for the night. She said that the shelter cooked dinner every night and gave it to the people who did not have any food or a place to live. My dad said that was why we were giving them food and why we had gone shopping. We were there so other people would have food to eat.

I now really look forward to going shopping for Thanksgiving. I try to pick the biggest turkey and the best potatoes. A few times a year my family cleans out our closets and gives old clothes, shoes, and blankets to the shelter. It still makes me sad to go to the shelter and see people standing in the cold and waiting for food, but I learned to be thankful for what I have and that it is really important to give to others.

How to Overcome Test Anxiety

Just the thought of taking a test is enough to make most people a little nervous. A test is an important event that can have a long-term impact on your future, so it's important to take it seriously and it's natural to feel anxious about performing well. But just because anxiety is normal, that doesn't mean that it's helpful in test taking, or that you should simply accept it as part of your life. Anxiety can have a variety of effects. These effects can be mild, like making you feel slightly nervous, or severe, like blocking your ability to focus or remember even a simple detail.

If you experience test anxiety—whether severe or mild—it's important to know how to beat it. To discover this, first you need to understand what causes test anxiety.

Causes of Test Anxiety

While we often think of anxiety as an uncontrollable emotional state, it can actually be caused by simple, practical things. One of the most common causes of test anxiety is that a person does not feel adequately prepared for their test. This feeling can be the result of many different issues such as poor study habits or lack of organization, but the most common culprit is time management. Starting to study too late, failing to organize your study time to cover all of the material, or being distracted while you study will mean that you're not well prepared for the test. This may lead to cramming the night before, which will cause you to be physically and mentally exhausted for the test. Poor time management also contributes to feelings of stress, fear, and hopelessness as you realize you are not well prepared but don't know what to do about it.

Other times, test anxiety is not related to your preparation for the test but comes from unresolved fear. This may be a past failure on a test, or poor performance on tests in general. It may come from comparing yourself to others who seem to be performing better or from the stress of living up to expectations. Anxiety may be driven by fears of the future—how failure on this test would affect your educational and career goals. These fears are often completely irrational, but they can still negatively impact your test performance.

Elements of Test Anxiety

As mentioned earlier, test anxiety is considered to be an emotional state, but it has physical and mental components as well. Sometimes you may not even realize that you are suffering from test anxiety until you notice the physical symptoms. These can include trembling hands, rapid heartbeat, sweating, nausea, and tense muscles. Extreme anxiety may lead to fainting or vomiting. Obviously, any of these symptoms can have a negative impact on testing. It is important to recognize them as soon as they begin to occur so that you can address the problem before it damages your performance.

The mental components of test anxiety include trouble focusing and inability to remember learned information. During a test, your mind is on high alert, which can help you recall information and stay focused for an extended period of time. However, anxiety interferes with your mind's natural processes, causing you to blank out, even on the questions you know well. The strain of testing during anxiety makes it difficult to stay focused, especially on a test that may take several hours. Extreme anxiety can take a huge mental toll, making it difficult not only to recall test information but even to understand the test questions or pull your thoughts together.

Effects of Test Anxiety

Test anxiety is like a disease—if left untreated, it will get progressively worse. Anxiety leads to poor performance, and this reinforces the feelings of fear and failure, which in turn lead to poor performances on subsequent tests. It can grow from a mild nervousness to a crippling condition. If allowed to progress, test anxiety can have a big impact on your schooling, and consequently on your future.

Test anxiety can spread to other parts of your life. Anxiety on tests can become anxiety in any stressful situation, and blanking on a test can turn into panicking in a job situation. But fortunately, you don't have to let anxiety rule your testing and determine your grades. There are a number of relatively simple steps you can take to move past anxiety and function normally on a test and in the rest of life.

Physical Steps for Beating Test Anxiety

While test anxiety is a serious problem, the good news is that it can be overcome. It doesn't have to control your ability to think and remember information. While it may take time, you can begin taking steps today to beat anxiety.

Just as your first hint that you may be struggling with anxiety comes from the physical symptoms, the first step to treating it is also physical. Rest is crucial for having a clear, strong mind. If you are tired, it is much easier to give in to anxiety. But if you establish good sleep habits, your body and mind will be ready to perform optimally, without the strain of exhaustion. Additionally, sleeping well helps you to retain information better, so you're more likely to recall the answers when you see the test questions.

Getting good sleep means more than going to bed on time. It's important to allow your brain time to relax. Take study breaks from time to time so it doesn't get overworked, and don't study right before bed. Take time to rest your mind before trying to rest your body, or you may find it difficult to fall asleep.

Along with sleep, other aspects of physical health are important in preparing for a test. Good nutrition is vital for good brain function. Sugary foods and drinks may give a burst of energy but this burst is followed by a crash, both physically and emotionally. Instead, fuel your body with protein and vitamin-rich foods.

Also, drink plenty of water. Dehydration can lead to headaches and exhaustion, especially if your brain is already under stress from the rigors of the test. Particularly if your test is a long one, drink water during the breaks. And if possible, take an energy-boosting snack to eat between sections.

Along with sleep and diet, a third important part of physical health is exercise. Maintaining a steady workout schedule is helpful, but even taking 5-minute study breaks to walk can help get your blood pumping faster and clear your head. Exercise also releases endorphins, which contribute to a positive feeling and can help combat test anxiety.

When you nurture your physical health, you are also contributing to your mental health. If your body is healthy, your mind is much more likely to be healthy as well. So take time to rest, nourish your body with healthy food and water, and get moving as much as possible. Taking these physical steps will make you stronger and more able to take the mental steps necessary to overcome test anxiety.

Mental Steps for Beating Test Anxiety

Working on the mental side of test anxiety can be more challenging, but as with the physical side, there are clear steps you can take to overcome it. As mentioned earlier, test anxiety often stems from lack of preparation, so the obvious solution is to prepare for the test. Effective studying may be the most important weapon you have for beating test anxiety, but you can and should employ several other mental tools to combat fear.

First, boost your confidence by reminding yourself of past success—tests or projects that you aced. If you're putting as much effort into preparing for this test as you did for those, there's no reason you should expect to fail here. Work hard to prepare; then trust your preparation.

Second, surround yourself with encouraging people. It can be helpful to find a study group, but be sure that the people you're around will encourage a positive attitude. If you spend time with others who are anxious or cynical, this will only contribute to your own anxiety. Look for others who are motivated to study hard from a desire to succeed, not from a fear of failure.

Third, reward yourself. A test is physically and mentally tiring, even without anxiety, and it can be helpful to have something to look forward to. Plan an activity following the test, regardless of the outcome, such as going to a movie or getting ice cream.

When you are taking the test, if you find yourself beginning to feel anxious, remind yourself that you know the material. Visualize successfully completing the test. Then take a few deep, relaxing breaths and return to it. Work through the questions carefully but with confidence, knowing that you are capable of succeeding.

Developing a healthy mental approach to test taking will also aid in other areas of life. Test anxiety affects more than just the actual test—it can be damaging to your mental health and even contribute to depression. It's important to beat test anxiety before it becomes a problem for more than testing.

Study Strategy

Being prepared for the test is necessary to combat anxiety, but what does being prepared look like? You may study for hours on end and still not feel prepared. What you need is a strategy for test prep. The next few pages outline our recommended steps to help you plan out and conquer the challenge of preparation.

Step 1: Scope Out the Test

Learn everything you can about the format (multiple choice, essay, etc.) and what will be on the test. Gather any study materials, course outlines, or sample exams that may be available. Not only will this help you to prepare, but knowing what to expect can help to alleviate test anxiety.

Step 2: Map Out the Material

Look through the textbook or study guide and make note of how many chapters or sections it has. Then divide these over the time you have. For example, if a book has 15 chapters and you have five days to study, you need to cover three chapters each day. Even better, if you have the time, leave an extra day at the end for overall review after you have gone through the material in depth.

If time is limited, you may need to prioritize the material. Look through it and make note of which sections you think you already have a good grasp on, and which need review. While you are studying, skim quickly through the familiar sections and take more time on the challenging parts.

Write out your plan so you don't get lost as you go. Having a written plan also helps you feel more in control of the study, so anxiety is less likely to arise from feeling overwhelmed at the amount to cover.

Step 3: Gather Your Tools

Decide what study method works best for you. Do you prefer to highlight in the book as you study and then go back over the highlighted portions? Or do you type out notes of the important information? Or is it helpful to make flashcards that you can carry with you? Assemble the pens, index cards, highlighters, post-it notes, and any other materials you may need so you won't be distracted by getting up to find things while you study.

If you're having a hard time retaining the information or organizing your notes, experiment with different methods. For example, try color-coding by subject with colored pens, highlighters, or post-it notes. If you learn better by hearing, try recording yourself reading your notes so you can listen while in the car, working out, or simply sitting at your desk. Ask a friend to quiz you from your flashcards, or try teaching someone the material to solidify it in your mind.

Step 4: Create Your Environment

It's important to avoid distractions while you study. This includes both the obvious distractions like visitors and the subtle distractions like an uncomfortable chair (or a too-comfortable couch that makes you want to fall asleep). Set up the best study environment possible: good lighting and a comfortable work area. If background music helps you focus, you may want to turn it on, but otherwise keep the room quiet. If you are using a computer to take notes, be sure you don't have any other windows open, especially applications like social media, games, or anything else that could distract you. Silence your phone and turn off notifications. Be sure to keep water close by so you stay hydrated while you study (but avoid unhealthy drinks and snacks).

Also, take into account the best time of day to study. Are you freshest first thing in the morning? Try to set aside some time then to work through the material. Is your mind clearer in the afternoon or evening? Schedule your study session then. Another method is to study at the same time of day that you will take the test, so that your brain gets used to working on the material at that time and will be ready to focus at test time.

Step 5: Study!

Once you have done all the study preparation, it's time to settle into the actual studying. Sit down, take a few moments to settle your mind so you can focus, and begin to follow your study plan. Don't give in to distractions or let yourself procrastinate. This is your time to prepare so you'll be ready to fearlessly approach the test. Make the most of the time and stay focused.

Of course, you don't want to burn out. If you study too long you may find that you're not retaining the information very well. Take regular study breaks. For example, taking five minutes out of every hour to walk briskly, breathing deeply and swinging your arms, can help your mind stay fresh.

As you get to the end of each chapter or section, it's a good idea to do a quick review. Remind yourself of what you learned and work on any difficult parts. When you feel that you've mastered the material, move on to the next part. At the end of your study session, briefly skim through your notes again.

But while review is helpful, cramming last minute is NOT. If at all possible, work ahead so that you won't need to fit all your study into the last day. Cramming overloads your brain with more information than it can process and retain, and your tired mind may struggle to recall even previously learned information when it is overwhelmed with last-minute study. Also, the urgent nature of cramming and the stress placed on your brain contribute to anxiety. You'll be more likely to go to the test feeling unprepared and having trouble thinking clearly.

So don't cram, and don't stay up late before the test, even just to review your notes at a leisurely pace. Your brain needs rest more than it needs to go over the information again. In fact, plan to finish your studies by noon or early afternoon the day before the test. Give your brain the rest of the day to relax or focus on other things, and get a good night's sleep. Then you will be fresh for the test and better able to recall what you've studied.

Step 6: Take a Practice Test

Many courses offer sample tests, either online or in the study materials. This is an excellent resource to check whether you have mastered the material, as well as to prepare for the test format and environment.

Check the test format ahead of time: the number of questions, the type (multiple choice, free response, etc.), and the time limit. Then create a plan for working through them. For example, if you have 30 minutes to take a 60-question test, your limit is 30 seconds per question. Spend less time on the questions you know well so that you can take more time on the difficult ones.

If you have time to take several practice tests, take the first one open book, with no time limit. Work through the questions at your own pace and make sure you fully understand them. Gradually work up to taking a test under test conditions: sit at a desk with all study materials put away and set a timer. Pace yourself to make sure you finish the test with time to spare and go back to check your answers if you have time.

After each test, check your answers. On the questions you missed, be sure you understand why you missed them. Did you misread the question (tests can use tricky wording)? Did you forget the information? Or was it something you hadn't learned? Go back and study any shaky areas that the practice tests reveal.

Taking these tests not only helps with your grade, but also aids in combating test anxiety. If you're already used to the test conditions, you're less likely to worry about it, and working through tests until you're scoring well gives you a confidence boost. Go through the practice tests until you feel comfortable, and then you can go into the test knowing that you're ready for it.

Test Tips

On test day, you should be confident, knowing that you've prepared well and are ready to answer the questions. But aside from preparation, there are several test day strategies you can employ to maximize your performance.

First, as stated before, get a good night's sleep the night before the test (and for several nights before that, if possible). Go into the test with a fresh, alert mind rather than staying up late to study.

Try not to change too much about your normal routine on the day of the test. It's important to eat a nutritious breakfast, but if you normally don't eat breakfast at all, consider eating just a protein bar. If you're a coffee drinker, go ahead and have your normal coffee. Just make sure you time it so that the caffeine doesn't wear off right in the middle of your test. Avoid sugary beverages, and drink enough water to stay hydrated but not so much that you need a restroom break 10 minutes into the test. If your test isn't first thing in the morning, consider going for a walk or doing a light workout before the test to get your blood flowing.

Allow yourself enough time to get ready, and leave for the test with plenty of time to spare so you won't have the anxiety of scrambling to arrive in time. Another reason to be early is to select a good seat. It's helpful to sit away from doors and windows, which can be distracting. Find a good seat, get out your supplies, and settle your mind before the test begins.

When the test begins, start by going over the instructions carefully, even if you already know what to expect. Make sure you avoid any careless mistakes by following the directions.

Then begin working through the questions, pacing yourself as you've practiced. If you're not sure on an answer, don't spend too much time on it, and don't let it shake your confidence. Either skip it and come back later, or eliminate as many wrong answers as possible and guess among the remaining ones. Don't dwell on these questions as you continue—put them out of your mind and focus on what lies ahead.

Be sure to read all of the answer choices, even if you're sure the first one is the right answer. Sometimes you'll find a better one if you keep reading. But don't second-guess yourself if you do immediately know the answer. Your gut instinct is usually right. Don't let test anxiety rob you of the information you know.

If you have time at the end of the test (and if the test format allows), go back and review your answers. Be cautious about changing any, since your first instinct tends to be correct, but make sure you didn't misread any of the questions or accidentally mark the wrong answer choice. Look over any you skipped and make an educated guess.

At the end, leave the test feeling confident. You've done your best, so don't waste time worrying about your performance or wishing you could change anything. Instead, celebrate the successful completion of this test. And finally, use this test to learn how to deal with anxiety even better next time.

Review Video: Test Anxiety
Visit mometrix.com/academy and enter code: 100340

Important Qualification

Not all anxiety is created equal. If your test anxiety is causing major issues in your life beyond the classroom or testing center, or if you are experiencing troubling physical symptoms related to your anxiety, it may be a sign of a serious physiological or psychological condition. If this sounds like your situation, we strongly encourage you to seek professional help.

Online Resources

Due to our efforts to try to keep this book to a manageable length, we've created a link that will give you access to all of your online resources:

mometrix.com/resources719/ssmstepg8ela

It's Your Moment, Let's Celebrate It!

Share your story @mometrixtestpreparation